COLLEGE
SECRETS

*How to Save Money, Cut College
Costs and Graduate Debt Free*

COLLEGE SECRETS

How to Save Money, Cut College Costs and Graduate Debt Free

By Lynnette Khalfani Cox

Advantage World Press

Published by Advantage World Press
An Imprint of TheMoneyCoach.net, LLC
P.O. Box 1307
Mountainside, NJ 07092

Book Packaging: Earl Cox & Associates Literary Management

ISBN 10: 1-932450-11-4
ISBN 13: 978-1-932450-11-8

LCCN: 2014947296

Publisher's Cataloging in Publication Data

Khalfani-Cox, Lynnette.

College secrets : how to save money, cut college costs and graduate debt free /
by Lynnette Khalfani Cox. -- First edition. -- Mountainside, NJ : Advantage World Press, [2015]

pages ; cm.

ISBN: 978-1-932450-11-8 ; 1-932450-11-4
Includes index.
Summary: "College Secrets" and its companion book, "College Secrets for Teens", reveal the true costs of earning a college degree, including hidden higher-education expenses. The author then provides hundreds of money-saving ideas to help students and parents reduce or eliminate these expenses, such as tuition costs, room and board expenses, activity fees, books and supplies, lifestyle costs, school surcharges and more. "College Secrets" also offers advice on obtaining scholarships, financial aid and student loans.--Publisher.

1. College costs--United States. 2. College students--United States--Finance, Personal. 3. Student loans--United States. 4. Student aid--United States. 5. Scholarships--United States. 6. Foreign study--Finance. 7. Saving and investment--United States. 8. Debt--United States. 9. Consumer credit--United States. 10. Finance, Personal--United States. I. Title.

LB2342 .K47 2015   2014947296
378.3/80973--dc23   1501

Printed in the United States of America

First Edition: 2015

SPECIAL SALES

Advantage World Press books are available at special bulk purchase discounts to use for sales promotions, premiums, or educational purposes. For more information, write to Advantage World Press, Special Markets, P.O. Box 1307, Mountainside, NJ 07092, or e-mail info@themoneycoach.net.

To my three amazing children,
Aziza, Jakada and Alexis.
You are the inspiration for all that I do.
I pray that college will inspire each of you
to reach your full potential.

To my incredibly wonderful husband, Earl.
You make my life so much better and so full of joy.
I pray that we'll stay as happy as we are today -- even
after paying for college.

OTHER BOOKS BY
LYNNETTE KHALFANI COX

ᴄᴛABLE OF ᴄᴏNTENTS

$\mathscr{I}$NTRODUCTION

Paying for college is a major challenge today — especially for students who don't want hefty college loans, and parents who don't want to sacrifice their retirement.

Unfortunately, the cost of a college education in the United States has skyrocketed to ridiculous levels. Over the past decade, higher education expenses have risen about 8% a year nationwide, driving the average price for a *public*, four-year college or university to its current cost of roughly $20,000 a year, including tuition, fees, room and board. The total average cost of a *private*, four-year institution now exceeds $40,000 annually, according to the data from the College Board.

At top colleges in America — including Ivy League schools, other elite, private institutions, and many excellent state schools that attract out-of-state students — it's common for total costs to hit the $50,000 to $60,000 range or more *per year*.

Not surprisingly, runaway college costs are taking a huge financial toll on families and sending scores of individuals into debt.

According to The Project on Student Debt, an initiative of The Institute for College Access & Success (TICAS), seven out of 10 college graduates in the U.S. now leave school with student loans averaging $29,400 per borrower. Mark Kantrowitz, a nationally recognized college expert who has crunched the very latest data available, says that borrowers who graduated in the Class of 2014 averaged $33,000 in student loans.

Cumulative college debt in America is also enormous, having tripled between 2004 and 2014, Federal Reserve data show. The total amount of student loans owed in the U.S. now exceeds ***$1.2 trillion,*** a mind-boggling amount of money.

And guess who's on the hook for most of those student loans?

If you think it's the 18-to-25-year-old crowd, or recent college grads, think again. Two-thirds of those who owe student loans are people age 30 *and older*.

A lot of these individuals graduated or left school a decade or more ago and are *still* repaying their college loans. Others returned to school mid-career and financed their degrees with student loans. And many borrowers weren't even students at all: they were *parents* who co-signed for their children's educational loans.

* * *

Our country's staggering $1.2 trillion in college debt is bad enough. But what is most troubling about these loans is that they are clearly unaffordable for millions of college grads and their parents.

Government statistics indicate that among borrowers in repayment, more than 30% are now 90 days or more delinquent on their student loans. Again, among those with past-due student loans, 67% of borrowers are age 30 *and older.*

This data doesn't even begin to account for parents who run up credit card debt, mortgage their homes, drain their retirement assets or take other drastic financial steps to pay for their kids' college expenses.

How has it come to this? And more importantly: how can you or your family avoid becoming a sad statistic in the quest for a college education?

Learning What No One Ever Taught You

By picking up this copy of *College Secrets*, you've taken a big step toward ensuring that college costs don't put you in the poorhouse.

College Secrets will provide you with an array of insights, hidden resources, little- known cost-cutting methods, and money-saving strategies that no one ever tells students and their parents — at least not in the comprehensive and step-by-step fashion that you'll find in this book.

I promise you this: by the time you finish reading *College Secrets*, you'll be armed with all the tools you need to successfully plan and pay for college — all without going broke.

The sad truth is that core financial literacy skills are not widely taught in America. There is no system in place to educate us about how to manage money. So is it any wonder that most people in this country are at a loss for how to best pay for big-ticket expenses like a college degree?

In fact, you could have already earned an MBA from one of the top colleges in the country, but chances are you never learned about something as basic and crucial as how to effectively pay for your (or your kid's) college education.

College Secrets will fix that problem. I guarantee it.

College Secrets is about to save you and your family a ton of money — anywhere from $5,000 to $50,000 *per year*.

I can make such a bold claim with confidence because I know the biggest college secret of all.

And here it is: For every college expense you'll encounter — and I mean *every single one* — there are multiple strategies to reduce or even eliminate your out-of-pocket costs. You just have to explore your options, use a little creativity, and resist the urge to simply whip out your checkbook or credit card every time you're asked.

Let me put this another way:

College Secret:

You can save a total of $20,000 to $200,000 during a four-year education just by being a smarter consumer.

* * *

Since you've taken the time to read this far, I assume that you likely fall into one of the following categories:

- You are a parent/guardian or relative of a college student or college-bound teen
- You are a high school student preparing for college
- You are a current college undergraduate
- You are a graduate student
- You are an adult considering returning to school
- You are a professional, such as a guidance counselor, financial aid officer, or a financial advisor and you want to help others make sound decisions

This book will help all of you — and allow you to share what you learn with others who are confronting the college financing dilemma.

The Importance of Financial Planning

Now I have to say a special word to parents/guardians and students:

I can't stress enough how important financial strategizing to lower college costs really is. That's what *College Secrets* is all about.

Too often, families don't get around to thinking about college costs until a son or daughter is well into high school, or even already in college. Some parents and their offspring only start to seriously consider higher education expenses once a college admissions package arrives that spells out what the school costs, as well as what college officials expect the family to contribute.

Fortunately, if you're a late starter — and most people are — you can still effectively manage college costs.

But make no mistake: the earlier you get started the better. Otherwise, too much procrastination and a lack of financial planning will wreak havoc on your family's budget when it's time to pay for college.

How do I know this?

The Money Coach is in Your Corner

As the co-founder of a free financial advice site, AskTheMoneyCoach. com, and a former financial journalist, I've spent the past 20 years helping millions of individuals, couples, and families to better manage their finances.

People come to AskTheMoneyCoach.com to pose questions about a range of personal finance topics and about situations they're facing: everything from getting out of debt or increasing their credit rating to investing wisely or obtaining the proper insurance to protect their assets and their loved ones.

I enjoy my work as a money coach because it gives me a chance to share my financial tips and advice in three primary ways: through my writing, speaking engagements, and in the media.

Some of you may have previously seen me quoted in national magazines or newspapers, or read my advice in my own articles, blog posts, and previous books.

Some of you may have attended one of my financial seminars or money-management workshops.

Or perhaps you've heard me on the radio or seen me as a guest expert on TV. I've appeared on numerous television programs, such as *The Today Show*; talk shows like *Oprah, Dr. Phil, The Talk, The Steve Harvey Show*; and on various news shows on CNN, MSNBC, FOX, ABC, and more.

I'm telling you all this to assure you that even if you've never heard of me until now, you can be confident that I'm a skilled financial educator who has helped scores of people — including many individuals just like you.

* * *

So how did I learn about this money stuff? Partly via my education and professional background, and partly through trial and error, better known as the school of hard knocks.

Before launching my own financial advice site in 2003, I was employed for nearly a decade at the global news powerhouse, Dow Jones & Co. In that capacity, I covered Wall Street as a Dow Jones Newswires reporter, served as a personal finance columnist and editor, and also worked as a *Wall Street Journal* reporter for CNBC.

I frequently tell people that my time at Dow Jones was "financial boot camp." I researched companies, learned about stocks and bonds, and interviewed some of the best and brightest minds on Wall Street. By doing so, I came to understand what it takes to get ahead financially — and what people do to set themselves back.

Why do I mention my financial journalism background?

It's simple. I want you to know that I'm not going to merely share my own opinions, insights and experiences with you.

College Secrets is the product of an exhaustive amount of research, plus interviews with college and money-management experts, guidance and financial aid counselors, parents, students, admissions officers and others.

In fact, even though consumers nationwide call me "The Money Coach," I often call myself "The Research Queen." I say that because I believe no one can out-research me when I'm determined to learn about a subject, and subsequently teach the nitty-gritty of the topic to others.

Just to let you in on a little secret of mine: When I was first researching this book, my oldest daughter frequently called me "OCD Mom," suggesting I suffered from obsessive-compulsive disorder.

She probably wasn't too far off.

Like some of you, I've become slightly obsessed (OK, more than slightly obsessed!) with learning the ins and outs of college and how to pay for it without going bankrupt.

I must confess that my interest in this subject isn't just professional curiosity. I have a huge *personal* interest in college planning, because, in addition to being a Money Coach, *I'm a parent just like many of you.*

In fact, like many of you, I'm a mom who is currently *deep* in the throes of college planning for my own three kids.

When I started seriously researching this book, my oldest daughter was a high school sophomore.

As of this writing, in August 2014, she's just about to enter her senior year in high school and we are actively engaged in getting her ready to start college in the fall of 2015. I also have two more children who will later attend college as well. My son is currently about to enter ninth grade and my youngest daughter is going into third grade.

So believe me when I say, dear parents (and you students too!) that I know what you're going through. College planning is a topic very near to my heart, personally and professionally.

But honestly, it's not important to me personally solely because I'm a mom. I also wish I'd known better, and had done many things differently when I was an undergrad and graduate student.

If I'd known back then what I know now, I wouldn't have come out of graduate school with $40,000 in student loans that took years to pay off.

My Personal College Story

I grew up in Los Angeles, and only applied to three colleges as a high school senior: University of California, Berkeley; University of California, Irvine; and Yale.

I got into the first two schools and was wait-listed at Yale. What I recall most was waiting anxiously for those admission decisions to arrive. Like most teens back then, I wanted to see big, thick envelopes land in my mailbox — a sure-fire sign of acceptance. Thin envelopes, we all knew, likely meant rejection.

These days, the process is entirely different. Many colleges now notify applicants online — via websites or email — about their admissions status.

And that's just the tip of the iceberg.

Remember how we fretted about the SAT, the primary admission test most colleges used to assess prospective students? Well, it was completely revamped in 2005. The exam previously had just two sections and a maximum score of 1,600 points. It now has three sections (math, writing and critical reading) for a total of 2,400 points. But guess what? The exam is changing yet again — going back to the old 1,600 point scoring system starting in the spring of 2016.

There's even greater pressure — right or wrong — for kids to score well on the SAT, the ACT, and other standardized exams to help them gain admission into certain colleges.

Some tests, such as the PSAT or Preliminary SAT (also known as the National Merit Scholarship Qualifying Test), can even help net students anywhere from $2,500 to the "Holy Grail" of college financial aid: a free "full ride," with all expenses paid at various institutions.

Given the staggering price tag of higher education today, the chance to get a "full ride" is no doubt appealing to many people.

It certainly was to me more than 20 years ago. Yet I turned down a "full ride" from an excellent graduate school in my early 20s (a decision I now regard as unwise on many fronts).

Turning Down a Full-Ride: Bold or Bone-Headed?

When I earned my undergraduate degree in 1991 from the University of California, Irvine, the total cost of attendance, including tuition, fees, room and board, was about $6,000 per year. That cost has now grown five-fold.

For the 2014-2015 school year, UCI charged $31,668 a year for in-state students living on campus and a whopping $54,546 annually for out-of-state students. (Costs at UC Berkeley, UCLA and other UC campuses are roughly comparable).

But it wasn't really my time as an undergraduate that got me into college debt. It was primarily two years of graduate school at a private institution where I amassed big student loans.

Upon completing my undergrad studies, I was accepted at both of the schools to which I applied: Boston University and the University of Southern California. But the admission and financial aid processes varied greatly at each school.

From the very start, I felt like Boston University was courting me heavily.

Admissions officers corresponded frequently and warmly with me. The university accepted me right away in the regular decision cycle, leaving no doubt that they wanted me to attend what was then the only double-major program in the country offering a Master's degree in both Journalism and African-American studies. Then came the icing on the cake: BU wowed me with very generous economic support to make my educational dreams a reality. Its offer amounted to more than $25,000 annually in free financial aid — essentially a "full ride" to pursue my graduate studies.

In contrast, by the time USC finally admitted me, I remember thinking, *What took so long?!* Admissions officials made me sweat it out for such an extended period that I was almost certain I was going to be rejected. So by the time that acceptance letter came, I guess I was feeling somewhat relieved, perhaps even grateful — at least until I read USC's aid package.

Unlike Boston University, USC's financial aid package was loaded primarily with student loans. Essentially, the school seemed to be saying: "You can come if you want, but you'll have to somehow foot nearly all of the bill."

I didn't know it at the time, but USC's offer was part of the rise of so-called "financial aid leveraging," a strategy that is all the rage now, despite some controversy over the practice.

Colleges use financial aid leveraging to attract those students a college finds most desirable (translation: rich kids or very high-scoring applicants) while simultaneously marginalizing and weeding out less desirable candidates (translation: poor students or those with less than stellar academic records). Leveraging is often done by diverting need-based financial aid away from lower-income students and giving merit-based, institutional aid to wealthier or high-achieving students.

And as a result of financial aid leveraging, I was being "gapped": offered admission, but with a financial aid offer that left a huge "gap" between USC's cost of attendance and my ability to pay for that school. The only way possible for me to attend USC, campus officials knew, was for me to go into debt in order to pay for that education.

Regrettably, I was all too willing to take out student loans, even though I was flat broke.

In hindsight, I am amazed that no family or friends really pressed me when I announced I was foregoing the full-ride at Boston University and opting instead to stay in the state and attend USC.

Honestly, I made the decision largely for personal reasons. I had been dating a man in Southern California and wanted to continue to the relationship. And when Boston University suddenly announced it was discontinuing the double-major program that intrigued me, that change gave me a convenient excuse to remain in L.A. and attend USC.

About a year later, I did marry that man I was seeing. In light of that, some of you may think: 'Aha! It was worth it to stay in Los Angeles.' Well maybe, maybe not. We subsequently moved to the East Coast, were married for 13 years, and then divorced.

I share this whole experience not to engage in a bit of TMI (too much information). I'm trying to point out:

1. The capriciousness of young people, and how many adolescents base school selection decisions on a whole host of things that really have nothing to do with the colleges themselves; and
2. The range of experiences the same student might get from two or more colleges, depending upon the institution's priorities, and how much (or how little) a college or university wants a particular student

Obviously, Boston U really wanted me. For a host of reasons, I was a very good fit for that campus, resulting in the school making me an aggressive offer. With USC, however, I clearly was not as desirable an applicant. Sure, I had the goods to get in. But there's a big difference between a school granting a student admission and then declining to provide that student with reasonable funding to make attendance possible.

Some people call the practice a form of "admit-deny."

"Admit-deny is when you give someone a financial-aid package that is so rotten that you hope they get the message: 'Don't come,'" Mark Heffron, a senior vice-president at Noel-Levitz, a large college consulting company, told The Atlantic magazine. Unfortunately, "they don't always get the message," he added.

In Chapter 9, I'll tell you more about financial aid strategies that colleges use — and how you can avoid certain pitfalls in order to maximize free aid from an institution.

Knowing what I now know, if any of my children ever tried to do the same thing I did and pass up a "full ride" to a great school — mainly so they could date someone — I would *strongly* encourage them to seriously reconsider.

Perhaps my choice was somewhat easier a few decades ago since college costs had not yet exploded to today's sky-high levels. Saying "no" to a $20,000 to $25,000 "full ride" back in the early 1990s was one thing. Today, however, it's harder to justify giving up a "full ride," which can total $40,000 to $60,000 or more annually. Yet, students still turn down such offers all the time.

Looking back at my overall education, my graduate school alma mater, USC, was a wonderful place to learn, and I really am grateful for the Master of Arts degree I earned in Journalism in 1993. I only regret the price tag.

That's because USC was pricey back then and it's just as pricey now, with a total annual cost of $65,111 for freshmen entering in 2014-2015.

Even so, USC received a record number of first-year applications for the fall of 2014 — 51,700 applicants in all — and the admission office admitted an all-time low of just 17.8% of those students.

Part of the school's appeal is no doubt USC's good reputation. But one factor in all those applications is also a major technological innovation that has greatly impacted the higher education application and admissions process. That innovation is the advent of the online Common Application.

In a nutshell: today's students can now fill out an electronic Common Application and instantly apply to as many as 20 schools. And believe it or not, many students do just that. With so many students seeking admission to a variety of colleges and universities, that means dramatically increased competition — not just for admission, but also for financial aid.

A New York Times article forecast that the number of applications filed through the Common Application portal by the end of this decade could exceed 10 million — and the number of schools accepting it could grow to 1,000 or more.

Don't let those statistics scare you, though. While the main focus of *College Secrets* is to teach people how to get through college without breaking the bank, I'll also share key admission tips that can help you get accepted into the college of your choice.

Before and after you get into your "dream" school, it's my hope that you'll refer to *College Secrets*, again and again, to use the "insider" strategies I share. These tried-and-true recommendations will help you cut costs, maximize financial aid, and best position yourself to save a bundle on higher education expenses.

But first: a word about how this book is organized.

A Quick Overview of *College Secrets*

College Secrets is broken into three distinct parts.

Part I covers upfront college costs, namely tuition, fees, room and board, as well as books and supplies. These are the "major" expenses that are typically top-of-mind for students and their parents. But they are far from the only college-related expenses you'll encounter. In fact, as I'll explain to you in this book, while tuition charges grab headlines and drive parents crazy with worry, a school's published tuition price is largely irrelevant. I realize that seems like a ridiculous notion — especially since you're contemplating paying the bill. But just stay with me, and I'll soon explain what I mean.

Part II covers hidden costs, which tend to be the real budget killers in paying for college. They include a slew of expenses — most of which the average student or parent hasn't planned for and often can't afford. So the focus of Part II is to make sure you don't get any nasty financial surprises once you or your child commits to attending an institution of higher learning.

In the first two parts of *College Secrets*, I'll not only clue you in on which expenses you should anticipate, I'll also give you a heads-up about which costs you *don't* need to worry about, and savvy ways to bypass certain pricey college items and activities that may initially seem like "must-haves."

Best of all: For each and every expense outlined in Parts I and II, I'll share with you a host of ways to save money. This advice represents the heart of *College Secrets*.

Part III explores financial aid strategies, which are crucial to all individuals interested in reducing college costs. I'll begin by examining tools that will help you forecast higher education expenses and help you stretch your dollars to gear up for paying for college, regardless of whether college bills are years away — or due right now. This section answers the gamut of frequently asked questions about college financial aid. I'll explain the financial aid process in detail, including the low-down on the FAFSA (or Free Application for Federal Student Aid), getting scholarships and grants, and understanding work-study opportunities that reduce your out-of-pocket expenses. Part III also provides you with detailed advice on how to pick the best student loans, just in case borrowing for college becomes a necessity.

* * *

Picking student loans would be a moot point for many families if only students picked the right college in the first place. The "right" college is the one that is the "best fit" for a student — academically, personally and financially. So if you're reading this book because you're a teenager, or you're a parent or guardian who wants to help prepare a teen that has not yet enrolled in college, I strongly encourage you to pick up a copy of the companion book in this series, called *College Secrets for Teens: Money Saving Ideas for the Pre-College Years*. It describes in detail how to pick the best college possible — and how to get into your first-choice college or university as well.

In *College Secrets for Teens*, one of the key insights I also share with students and families is that college costs don't just begin once a person goes off to campus as a first-year student. In fact, you'll start shelling out significant money for higher education long before you or your kid ever receives a college acceptance letter.

So *College Secrets for Teens* covers pre-college expenses in great detail. It includes everything from what you can expect to pay while going on college visits, to how much you'll likely fork over for college admissions tests, exam prep and college applications. I walk you through pre-college and summer programs, and other pre-college activities that can help prepare you for college, but that typically cost money. And just like with this book, for each expense outlined in *College Secrets for Teens*, I'll share with you a host of ways to save money. I believe *College Secrets for Teens* is crucial for high school (and even middle school) students and their parents.

Whether you're a student with a younger sibling who has not yet entered college, or a parent planning ahead for a young child, you may want to read *College Secrets for Teens*, pass along the tips you learn, and then give that book to your younger family member. Trust me: you'll be doing him or her an enormous favor.

Throughout the *College Secrets* series, I'll share strategies and insights that cover special circumstances, in recognition that there are a slew of different scenarios confronting various readers. Some of you may come from low-income households, while others of you may be wealthier international students, transfer applicants, undocumented students or the first in your family to attend college.

Still others may want information based on their specific demographic traits, such as minority heritage, ethnicity, or even status as a foster or adopted child. Both books in the *College Secrets* series offer money-saving tips for individuals with all these special circumstances and more.

Ultimately, the *College Secrets* series will become your roadmap to financing a college education the proper way — with some sanity, knowledge and planning in the process, and without going broke or winding up deep in debt.

* * *

Unfortunately, most students — and their parents — tackle college planning the wrong way. They focus almost exclusively on trying to gain admission into a "dream school," and then they worry later about how to actually *pay* for college.

In my view, that's an ill-advised strategy and one that can put a family in the poorhouse. A better approach is to handle financial issues first and foremost as part of the process when selecting a college that's the best possible fit academically, personally, and financially.

But don't worry. I don't suggest that you pick a school based solely on tuition, or that you exclude certain colleges simply based on economics.

Rather, in the *College Secrets* series, I'll show you how mastering the financial aspect of college — *before* falling in love with a campus or even applying to a single school — is the most prudent way to help pick an institution that's the best possible fit.

My approach takes a multitude of factors into account — including financial factors you may not have considered. In this way, you make college financing an overall part of the college selection, application and admission processes. You do that by taking a realistic look at the true overall price of college, including pre-college expenses, upfront costs, and hidden costs, too.

The net result is that you (or your child) will find a terrific school. More importantly, that school will likewise want you — and the college will *prove* its interest by being supportive with grant aid, scholarships, and private or institutional funds that don't have to be repaid.

In other words, your financial aid package should invoke feelings that are closer to the sentiments I had after getting Boston University's offer, and not the feelings I had after receiving USC's offer.

I hope you're as excited to go on this journey, as I am to be your guide. So if you're ready, let's get started!

PART I

UPFRONT
COLLEGE COSTS

CHAPTER 1

⟨T⟩UITION AND ⟨F⟩EES

If you or one of your children has recently received a college acceptance letter, or if you're already a college student continuing your education, congratulations! Even if college is a couple years off, it's time to figure out how to pay a host of upfront college bills.

When you think about college costs, what's the very first thing that comes to mind? For most people, tuition and fees top the list.

Escalating tuitions grab headlines and often strikes fear into the hearts of students and parents who know they can't possibly foot such massive college bills alone.

But you need not lose sleep over exorbitant, scary-sounding tuition prices, because over the next two chapters, I'll tell you 24 ways to drastically cut tuition expenses and keep your budget intact.

The Truth About College Tuition

Before I reveal those strategies, however, it's important to first understand three key concepts about college tuition.

1. College tuition is largely irrelevant
2. College tuition is no indication of college quality
3. College tuition doesn't always go where you think

Let's begin with my first claim. Don't close the book and think I'm batty. Please keep reading and bear with me while I explain what I mean and why it's the God's honest truth.

What's Tuition Got to Do With It?

A lot of the fretting and handwringing by students and parents over tuition and fees is largely misplaced angst. In fact, one of the least understood secrets of paying for higher education is that in many ways college tuition is largely irrelevant.

I know this assertion may seem counterintuitive, perhaps even baffling or ridiculous. But for many reasons, it's an enormous mistake to focus on a college's published tuition price when you're trying to effectively manage total college costs.

For starters, according to the College Board's latest Trends in College Pricing report, tuition and fees account for only 39% of the total expenses paid by in-state college students enrolled in public four-year institutions. That means the remaining 61% of costs — a big majority — were actually *non-tuition* expenses. The biggest out-of-pocket cost for many students is actually living expenses. So if anything, that's the category of expenditures where students and parents need to be most concerned.

Evaluating colleges and higher education costs based mainly on tuition also leaves you vulnerable to the financial tricks that some colleges play. For example, to avoid student backlash over annual tuition hikes, some institutions may raise tuition prices only slightly or perhaps not at all. Meanwhile, those same campus officials are drastically boosting other costs. If you're not careful about such shenanigans, and you take your eyes off all *other* rising expenses, you'll wind up forking over a lot of unanticipated money — far more than the tuition hikes you so desperately feared.

Here's another practical reason that you shouldn't needlessly sweat over tuition prices. Relatively few students actually pay a college or university's published tuition price. On average, U.S. colleges discount their stated tuition rates by about 44%, the National Association of College and University Business Officers says. Colleges discount tuition by providing students with institutional funds — like grants and scholarships — that don't have to be repaid. Some institutions even routinely knock off 50% or so of the tuition bill.

"At private four-year schools, students are paying about half the sticker price," says Lucie Lapovsky, an economist and expert in higher education finance, who is also the former president of Mercy College.

From the standpoint of finding the best college fit, ruling out certain institutions just based on their stated tuition often leads to poor college decision-making. But scores of students do this all the time. In fact, a whopping 60% of students rule a school out based on price alone, data from Sallie Mae shows. One by-product of that knee-jerk reaction to price is that high achieving low-income and middle-class students who focus excessively on college tuition often "undermatch" and fail to even apply to the top schools for which they are academically qualified. These same institutions typically have greater resources and offer better financial aid, making their net costs more affordable.

For example, consider an outstanding, first generation student of modest means living in New Jersey. That student may automatically assume that his or her state school, Rutgers University, will be a better bargain than Princeton University, because Rutgers' 2014-2015 basic tuition price was $10,954 at its main New Brunswick campus, while Princeton's hit $41,820, almost four times Rutgers' price. What this student probably won't consider, however, is that his or her out-of-pocket expenses are likely to be lower at Princeton than many public schools. Thanks to a huge endowment and generous financial aid policies, Princeton can afford to offer substantial need-based aid that doesn't have to be repaid. For example, the average financial aid grant at Princeton covers 100% of tuition, and the school has a "no loan" policy in awarding financial aid.

As previously mentioned, no matter what a school's sticker price, there are a multitude of strategies that students and their families can use to either greatly reduce tuition costs, or in some cases eliminate tuition all together.

So believe me when I say that it's to your advantage to understand that college tuition shouldn't be the sole financial consideration in your college selection process. School tuition is just the tip of the iceberg. My advice: Know how to cut tuition, of course. But don't just focus on tuition; scrutinize everything else. By understanding this concept, you'll fare much better in finding the right institution for you and managing total college costs.

College Tuition Does Not Equal College Quality

We've all heard the expression "You get what you pay for." The notion behind this concept is that if you want something of "better" quality, you have to pay more for it. This idea also suggests that anything you can obtain free of charge probably isn't of equal value to something for which money was paid.

Well, the old adage "you get what you pay for" might be true when it comes to cars, clothes or even day-old cookies given away by your local grocer. But this concept is dead wrong when it comes to college pricing, especially college tuition.

To begin with, Lapovsky says the price of college (i.e. what you pay to attend the school) and the cost of college (i.e. what it actually costs to provide your education), are not highly correlated. Furthermore, the net revenue from tuition is not generally indicative of the institution's costs, either.

That's one reason why Lapovsky says that no matter what a school's "sticker price" or published cost, "families should focus on net price," or what their specific out-of-pockets costs will be.

As it turns out, your net price can vary dramatically from one school to another, or it may be identical — even between two schools of vastly different quality. This strongly suggests that college tuition alone bears little to no resemblance to the quality of education one receives.

Despite an abundance of evidence to the contrary, plenty of parents think that if a school is super-expensive, it must be a really good school. But that simply isn't the case. One school could be more "expensive" for you, simply because your net costs are greater. But that doesn't make the school any better.

There are more than 2,200 non-profit, four-year colleges in America, including many low-cost institutions that offer an excellent education. Likewise, there are some high-priced schools that do a poor job of graduating students on time and teaching young adults the fundamentals they'll need to succeed. So don't buy into the notion that expensive schools are always somehow "better" than cheaper options.

If you're not quite convinced, consider this scenario:

When two college students pursue a similar degree at the exact same state school, yet one person is an in-state resident and the other individual is an out-of-state student, the out-of-state student typically winds up paying tuition that is two to three times higher than his in-state peer.

In spite of the cost difference in tuition, both individuals received identical instruction. Paying more money didn't get the out-of-state student a better education.

So it behooves you to truly understand that college costs do *not* equate with college quality.

The fact is that colleges consistently raise prices in large part because they can. The demand is there for them to do so. But once enough parents stop associating high cost with high quality, and increased competition comes to the educational arena, you'll find college costs stabilizing and even decreasing.

A Hard Question for Parents

How many of you have adopted an unhealthy "whatever it takes" mentality when it comes to paying for college?

Probably more of you than you would care to admit.

I've heard the stories from desperate parents who borrow from their retirement accounts, max out their credit cards, and do all sorts of other things to "afford" college costs.

In fact, a Sallie Mae survey shows that about 60% of parents and students alike say they are "willing to stretch financially" for college.

Among some parents, in our eagerness to send our sons and daughters to "the best schools that money can buy," we've sacrificed in ways large and small. Most damaging, we've continued to unwisely borrow staggering sums of money for higher education, showing colleges and universities nationwide that they can hike their prices and that we'll continue to bear the burden of those increases.

Unfortunately, this "sacrifice at all costs" strategy backfires on us in multiple ways.

First, we get stuck with higher college bills for four or more years. Additionally, we often become saddled with debt, especially student loans that either we or our children are forced to repay for a decade or more. Finally, we feed the college pricing frenzy by showing a willingness to pay more or borrow more.

Put another way: what many parents don't realize is that they're inadvertently adding to the mania in college pricing. Believe it or not, some schools have been known to raise their prices simply to elevate their prominence in the eyes of ill-informed families. These institutions know that many parents mistakenly view price as a proxy for quality. It's a sad and vicious cycle, and one that ensnares far too many unsuspecting families.

"The world of college is a business and schools price themselves accordingly," says college expert Lynn O'Shaughnessy, who runs a popular blog called The College Solution and has authored a book by the same name. "It's about supply and demand. The schools that have the greatest demand can charge the highest prices, and many of these schools will have poorer financial aid."

"The Ivy League schools and the alpha dogs of the college world — like Amherst, Williams, MIT or Stanford — do give very good financial aid, but many students at those campuses also pay full price," she adds. "The reason rich students flock there is they think it's their golden ticket."

Why Employers Don't Care Where You Went to School

Please realize that graduating from a prestigious school with a big sticker price and large tuition expenses won't be a magic ticket to a great job — nor a successful, happy future.

According to a survey conducted by Gallup and released by the Lumina Foundation, the vast majority of hiring managers really don't care where a job candidate went to school.

Corporate bosses were far more interested in a job applicant's knowledge and experience when determining whom to hire.

Unfortunately, most people get it wrong on this front, too — mistakenly assuming that employers want to see a brand name institution on a person's resume.

In that Gallup survey, 80% of Americans polled said that school choice is either "very important" (30%) or "somewhat important" (50%) to hiring managers.

Thank goodness that business leaders actually say just the opposite — and they're the ones making the hiring decisions.

Among business leaders surveyed, just 9% said that where a job candidate earned his or her degree is "very important," and 37% said it is "somewhat important."

All of this illustrates that you don't need to pick a pricey school or a name-brand campus just because you think it will automatically make you a more attractive job applicant. In most cases, it won't.

Your College Tuition Isn't Going Where You Think

When you see that at many top public colleges' total costs in America exceed $25,000 annually, and that costs for many excellent private schools are in the $50,000 to $60,000 range or more *per year*, it's quite mind-blowing.

Does it cost good money for schools of all kinds to hire and retain excellent faculty, build or maintain nice facilities, or put on any number of campus programs? Of course it does.

But do those expenses justify the aggressive year-over-year price increases witnessed this past decade? Absolutely not!

Fortunately, when you see the advertised price for a given college, that's just the sticker price. Most families don't pay published tuition rates. Scholarships, grants, and other financial aid help offset those costs.

But just knowing how much college costs have escalated is a real eye-opener to many parents.

If that's not enough, here's another wake-up call.

You might think that most of your tuition dollars are going toward salaries for professors and activities that provide a direct benefit to education. Well, that assumption would be misguided — not to mention a bit naïve and ill-informed.

Economist Rudy Fichtenbaum is a professor at Wright State University, Fairborn, Ohio, and president of the American Association of University Professors. In an interview with the Wall Street Journal, he decried the amount of money being spent not on professor salaries, but on a whole host of other things.

"Critics of higher education often blame faculty salaries for rising costs. However, when measured in constant dollars, salaries for full-time faculty at public institutions have actually declined," Fichtenbaum said. "What is driving costs (are) the metastasizing army of administrators with bloated salaries, and our university presidents who are now paid as though they were CEOs running a business — and not a very successful one at that."

"There is also the growth in entertainment spending and spending on amenities. Many universities claim that they must compete and therefore have borrowed millions to build luxury dorms, new dining halls and rock-climbing walls. They also spend millions subsidizing intercollegiate athletics," he added.

Some students take advantage of these "amenities"; others don't. But the reality is that everyone pays for them — unless you know better.

Tuition dollars are diverted in other ways you may not expect.

A separate Wall Street Journal report in 2014 highlighted how some students' tuition payments are subsidizing their classmates' tuition. According to the Journal, due to cutbacks in state aid, at least a dozen flagship state schools take tuition payments made by middle class families and wealthy families and use that tuition revenue to cover tuition for low-income students. These so-called "tuition set-asides" have grown dramatically in recent years. The Journal's analysis found that at public schools, tuition set-asides range from 5% to 40% of college tuition that students pay. Meanwhile, at private schools without large endowments, more than half of the tuition payments may be set aside for financial-aid scholarships. At both public and private colleges and universities, school officials use tuition set-aides as a way to create a more diverse student body and to meet various institutional goals.

An NPR report in 2014 offered an even more detailed, fascinating account of where tuition dollars are spent at private postsecondary schools.

NPR examined Duke University, an elite institution that had tuition and fees of $45,620 in 2013-2014. The total cost of attendance at Duke — including tuition, fees, room and board — was $61,404 in 2013-2014. In profiling the campus, NPR quoted Duke executive vice provost Jim Roberts as saying that students paying full freight — or just over $60,000 annually — were still actually getting a substantial "discount" off their education.

How is this even remotely possible?

In a nutshell, school officials say that it takes about $90,000 a year to educate a student at Duke. Of that total, here's a breakdown of how the money gets spent:

- $21,000, or 23%, goes to faculty compensation
- $20,000, or 22%, goes to Duke students who get financial aid
- $14,000, or 16%, goes to pay a share of administrative and academic support salaries, (including more than $1 million in total compensation to Duke's president and more than $500,000 to the provost)
- 14,000, or 16%, goes to dorms, food and health services
- $8,000, or 8%, goes into building and maintaining physical infra-structure
- $7,000, or 8%, goes to staff salaries for deans and faculty
- $5,000, or 7%, goes to miscellaneous costs

It should be noted that at Duke, about 53% of the student body pays the full, published sticker price, in excess of $60,000 annually.

For the record, NPR wasn't picking on Duke — and neither am I in highlighting these statistics. After all, among top-ranking schools, Duke isn't alone in having such costs. You'll find similar expenses from many of its private-school peers. Nor is Duke unique among elite research univer-sities and prestigious liberal arts colleges in claiming that you're getting a relative bargain if you fork over about a quarter of a million dollars over four years to earn a Bachelor's degree.

So if you want to worry about tuition — that is, tuition that you actually have to pay out of pocket, not a school's stated tuition price — perhaps the first question to ask a school is: *how exactly will my tuition dollars be spent?*

If you're happy with the answers, and you later decide to pay up, then the obvious question you have to ask yourself is: *will it ultimately be worth it?*

At the end of this chapter, I'll share the story of a Duke alumna who answers that question. Later on in Chapter 9 of *College Secrets*, I'll also tell you other key financial questions you should always pose to any school you're seriously considering.

But right now, you may be wondering about tuition allocation at some of the country's best *public* colleges and universities.

As of this writing, a direct comparison between Duke and its in-state rival, the University of North Carolina at Chapel Hill, another stellar institution, isn't available. That's because Carolina has not previously disclosed how tuition for residents (which was $8,340 in 2013-2014) was spent. Starting in the 2014-2015 academic year, however, all UNC campuses will begin providing tuition breakdowns to students.

So at this point, let's compare Duke with another top-ranking state school, the University of Texas at Austin, which currently breaks down the $9,346 in yearly tuition that some liberal arts students pay, as follows:

Category	Amount	Percentage
Instructional Salaries	$1377.00	29.5%
Staff Salaries	$669.66	14.3%
Employee Health Benefits	$675.44	14.5%
Other Operating	$515.41	11%
Utilities	$197.38	4.2%
Scholarships	$421.89	9%
Debt & Capital	$134.69	2.9%
Student Services	$681.53	14.6%

NOTE: Since the chart above only accounts for one semester, I multiplied the total figure of $4,673 by two to come up with the annual tuition cost of $9,346.

By way of reference, here are two other charts, also provided by UT Austin, illustrating 2013-2014 tuition for both residents and non-residents attending top public institutions in America.

2013-14 Tuition/Total Undergraduate Academic Costs for Residents (for fall and spring semesters)

Institution	Rank by Cost	Total Academic Cost: Resident
Pennsylvania State University-University Park	1	$16,992
University of Illinois at Urbana-Champaign	2	$15,258
University of California-Berkeley	3	$14,878
University of California-San Diego	4	$14,721
University of California-Los Angeles	5	$14,227
University of Minnesota-Twin Cities	6	$13,555
University of Michigan-Ann Arbor	7	$13,142
Michigan State University	8	$12,863
University of Washington	9	$12,397
University of Wisconsin-Madison	10	$10,403
Indiana University-Bloomington	11	$10,209
Ohio State University-Main Campus	12	$10,037
Purdue University	13	$9,992
University of Texas at Austin	14	$9,798*
University of North Carolina at Chapel Hill	15	$8,340

2013-14 Total Undergraduate Academic Costs for Non-residents (for fall and spring semesters)

Institution	Rank by Cost	Total Academic Cost: Non-resident
University of Michigan-Ann Arbor	1	$40,392
University of California-Berkeley	2	$37,756
University of California-San Diego	3	$37,599
University of California-Los Angeles	4	$37,105
University of Texas at Austin	5	$33,842
Michigan State University	6	$33,750
Indiana University-Bloomington	7	$32,350
University of Washington	8	$31,971
University of North Carolina at Chapel Hill	9	$30,122
University of Illinois at Urbana-Champaign	10	$29,640
Pennsylvania State University-University Park	11	$29,566
Purdue University	12	$28,794
University of Wisconsin-Madison	13	$26,653
Ohio State University-Main Campus	14	$25,757
University of Minnesota-Twin Cities	15	$19,805

Source: University of Texas at Austin website; data retrieved May 2014 http://www.utexas.edu/tuition/national.html

*Note: University of Texas at Austin rates are based on figures as reported to the Texas Higher Education Coordinating Board and represent the average academic year cost for a resident undergraduate student taking 30 credit hours per academic year.

So here's the bottom line: when students or parents have to actually foot the total bill for tuition (and most don't), each family must decide for itself whether a school that charges, say, $45,000 for tuition is truly twice or even three times as good as institutions charging roughly $22,500, or colleges charging about $15,000 or less.

Needless to say, there is no unanimity on this topic — especially from former students.

* * *

Jaclyn Vargo is a Harvard University graduate, who started off as a pre-med student before switching fields and majoring in social anthropology. She left Harvard with a small amount of student loans.

Before and during her time at Harvard, Vargo competed in U.S. Figure Skating.

Both areas "exposed me to a class of people I would not have known existed — the 1%," Vargo says.

"There were people whose parents were high-powered investment bankers and doctors, and those students had private drivers that would bring them to the skating rink. I grew up in the Catskills near Monticello where you had to go to the post office to get your mail," she recalls.

But after performing well both on and off the ice, and acing various standardized tests, including New York state's Regents exams, Vargo says, "I could directly compare my academic success with them and it made me realize I could be successful and that they were no better than I was."

Vargo competed at the U.S. championships at the junior level. She knew early on that she wanted to have a long-term affiliation with professional skating, so she started trial judging on her 16th birthday, and got her first appointment on her 18th birthday.

Vargo says she appreciates her undergraduate experiences at Harvard, but she also believes that too many students go into debt because they are blinded by brand names when picking potential schools. "You think you're set if you go to a certain school. But that is definitely not the case," she says. "I don't think Ivy League schools or other top schools like Hamilton or Middlebury are the key to success. In fact, I think it can really hinder you if you walk away with a ton of debt," Vargo says.

After Harvard, Vargo received her J.D. from Fordham Law School in 2003, where she was Editor-in-Chief of the Fordham Intellectual Property, Media & Entertainment Law Journal.

Upon finishing her schooling, Vargo served eight years as an Assistant District Attorney in New York County where she was a member of the Public Assistance Fraud and Domestic Violence units. Even while pursuing her law career, skating was never far from Vargo's life. She received her national judging appointment and was honored to judge at the 2007 U.S. Figure Skating Championships, becoming the first African-American to sit on a panel at that event.

In 2011, Vargo became the Associate Director of Career Services and Diversity Initiatives at Brooklyn Law School, a position she held for several years.

Then in March 2014, Vargo joined the New York State Gaming Commission, where she's now Assistant Counsel and Ethics Officer. She's also the National Chair of the Ethics Committee for U.S. Figure Skating, and a happily married mom of two young children.

Vargo's message to students today is simple: Hard work and discipline are what count the most. "The college you attend is not a magic bullet," she says. "You can be successful no matter what."

Vargo's story is just one out of many from students who have graduated from America's most esteemed colleges and universities.

Other alumni say the pricier tuition at top colleges is worth the cost because of the resources and opportunities that elite schools offer.

For instance, Yunha Kim, a Duke alumna from the Class of 2011, credits the campus with helping her in numerous ways — including building her confidence, giving her international business exposure and even aiding her post-school efforts as a budding entrepreneur.

"My parents paid for my education and Duke was expensive. But it was definitely worth it. If I had to go to school again, I'd go back to Duke," says Kim, who was born in Korea.

Kim says she was a shy teenager when she came to the United States, and attended a boarding school in Oregon.

At Duke, she majored in Economics and Chinese.

"I did four study-abroad programs while at Duke because I really wanted to leverage that time. I went to Florence, London, Beijing and New

York to study. That helped me to understand different cultures and people's work styles, and to become more confident," Kim says.

"That was the best part of my learning experience at Duke. It was about the discipline and interacting with really driven people. At Duke, people were always talking about their passion, so it was great being in an environment where people were super excited about their work and had clear goals."

Kim recalls a time when she was traveling with her parents in Florida and her car was vandalized. "They stole all my stuff, including my laptop," she says. After the incident, she told one of her Duke professors what happened and Kim explained that, unfortunately, she was not able to do her homework as a result of the theft.

"He was so understanding. He said 'I have another laptop.' Then he just gave it to me. That kind of personal care really goes far," she says.

Kim spent her college summers interning at McKinsey & Company and the United Nations before going on to land her first job at Jefferies as an investment banking analyst in the healthcare group.

Despite having good pay, nice colleagues and challenging work, it didn't take long for Kim to realize that banking wasn't her true passion.

So in March 2013, she quit her Jefferies job and started a Silicon Valley startup company called Locket, an Android lock screen application company that shows you ads and other content on your lock screen right before you unlock your smart-phone. Locket replaces your boring, standard lock screen images with stories and photos that you like, based on your interests, swiping habits, and the time of day.

"It's been going really well. We're always changing and evolving our product," Kim says. Best of all, she adds: "I'm having so much more fun than before. I'm learning a lot. But because I *want* to do this, I'm more actively learning."

Since she's operating in the male-dominated tech world, Kim tries to take nothing for granted. She's written about the pros and cons of being a young female running a technology start-up.

Kim is also quick to acknowledge that she's leveraged her Duke connections.

To raise capital, "I started by pulling out the directory of Duke alumni, and I would just call everyone one by one," Kim says. "Then Duke professors and alumni I didn't even know introduced me to investors. That's when I realized that this college education I got, that was so expensive, has given me huge returns."

Sure enough, the first round of funding that Kim secured for Locket was from Duke alumni. More investors followed in late 2013 and 2014. Among them: Fierce Capital, LLC, the investment arm of The Tyra Banks Company. Locket has reportedly raised millions so far from a cadre of diverse investors.

"When you're paying for tuition," Kim says, "you're also investing in your personal network and what happens outside of classes."

The experiences shared by Vargo and Kim offer two insightful yet different perspectives on the relative merits of attending top U.S. educational institutions — and paying for them.

Now that you have a better framework for understanding what is happening with college tuition all across America, let's turn to exploring two dozen strategies that will help you lower tuition costs — no matter what type of school you decide to attend.

CHAPTER 2

16 TUITION-BUSTING STRATEGIES ALL STUDENTS MUST KNOW

Thinking ahead and forming a plan to reduce tuition and other college costs is essential to managing higher education expenses. Such planning will also keep you from going into debt — or simply sticking your head in the sand and praying for the best.

"You can not just trust that paying for college will work itself out," says college consultant Peter Van Buskirk, who runs BestCollegeFit.com. "If you were going to invest in a quarter million dollar property, would you sign the papers without knowing upfront how your financing was going to work out?"

Of course you wouldn't. So you shouldn't leave higher education financing to chance, either. After all, college is quickly becoming the biggest investment that many families make — right up there with the cost of buying a new home.

* * *

Sixteen specific tuition-reduction strategies apply to all students. They are:

1. Go to a "no tuition" college
2. Get a tuition discount — or negotiate a larger one
3. Go overseas for college

4. Use the two-step college option
5. Attend a college with fixed-price tuition
6. Seek tuition waivers
7. Earn a degree in three years
8. Get tuition breaks based on your parents
9. Take advantage of in-state bargains
10. Take summer courses
11. Prepay college expenses
12. Tap into pipeline programs
13. Attend a work college
14. Get your employer to pay
15. Work in a high-need field and get the college to pay
16. Find a college with a guarantee program

1. Go to a "No Tuition" College

Even though the vast majority of U.S. colleges and universities do charge tuition, there are about a dozen schools in America that are classified as so-called "tuition free" or "no tuition" institutions.

If you get accepted into one of these schools, your worries about tuition can be put to rest. These schools forgo tuition dollars because they want their students to pursue higher education without excessive qualms about money. They also don't want students to be riddled with college debt upon graduation.

But be warned: even if you attend a "no tuition" school, you still typically have other college expenses to contend with, like housing, meals, books and supplies.

You should also know that competition to get into many tuition-free schools is fierce, and some schools require that students possess special talents.

For instance, musically gifted applicants might want to seek admission to the Curtis Institute of Music in Philadelphia, a prestigious conservatory that covers all tuition costs for each of its talented students. Curtis offers programs of study in a range of areas, including Brass, Guitar, Strings and Vocal Studies. The school even loans Steinway grand pianos to all students majoring in Composition, Conducting, Harpsichord and Piano.

Meanwhile, Barclay College, a 4-year Bible college, provides a full tuition scholarship to every accepted student who enrolls at its Haviland, Kansas campus. The school offers a Christian-centered education with undergraduate degrees in Business Administration, Elementary Education, Pastoral Ministry, Psychology, Theology, and more.

Undergraduates interested in architecture, art or engineering might look at Cooper Union in New York City. During the 2013-2014 academic year, Cooper Union charged no tuition to its undergraduates, but in the wake of the Great Recession, the school did begin charging tuition to its small group of graduate students. According to its website, Cooper Union will award half tuition scholarships to all incoming students starting in the fall of 2014. The school also promises to award merit aid to "exceptional students" and to provide need-based aid to low-income students "to help cover tuition, housing, food, books, supplies, etc."

America's service academies represent another form of "no tuition" higher education institutions. These storied institutions include the Air Force, Coast Guard, Military and Naval academies. In exchange for agreeing to serve their country for five years, students who get into these elite schools pay no tuition and get living stipends as well.

On the international front, there's even an institution called University of the People, which bills itself as the world's first tuition-free online university. Supported by software behemoth Microsoft, this U.S. accredited, non-profit school has a scholarship program to mentor, train and ultimately provide jobs to promising young adults across the African continent. The university was launched in November 2013 as part of Microsoft's 4Afrika Initiative. The school taps Microsoft employees around the world who provide students with leadership and technical training in computer science and business administration.

University of the People is affiliated with the United Nations, the Clinton Global Initiative, New York University and the Yale Law School Information Society Project.

Applicants must be at least 18 years old, possess a high-school diploma or the equivalent, and have reliable Internet access. By mid-2014, the school had already registered online students from more than 140 countries around the globe.

2. Go Overseas For a Cheaper Degree

Of course online schools aren't the only way to attend a tuition-free international school. In some countries, such as Germany, tuition is free for all college students.

That's why if you do decide to study abroad, you certainly won't be alone.

About 46,000 U.S. students are enrolled in full-degree programs outside the country, according to a data from the Institute of International Education's Project Atlas. Many of these students are no doubt enticed by lower tuition costs or even free tuition abroad in various countries.

Since tuition around the globe is either free or low-cost compared to the U.S., students often find that they still spend less for a degree overseas, even after factoring in housing, travel and other college costs.

Even if you have to pay slightly higher tuition rates at an out-of-country college or university than your peers abroad must pay, that tuition will still be much lower than college prices in America.

For those who need monetary help, in many instances you can even still access U.S. financial aid programs while you're studying elsewhere. The U.S. Department of Education has approved some 400 colleges and universities overseas to participate in its Title IV federal student aid programs. To find out if a school you're interested in is eligible, just use the FAFSA's Federal School Code Search tool to locate the school's federal code. (In the menu of this tool, change the setting from "state" to "foreign country.")

Another bonus: many overseas programs last just three years, instead of four years as is the case in America. A three-year program lets you save money all around and get to work a lot faster if you're eager to start a career.

So how can you explore this option?

Not all foreign universities accept the Common Application, so you may need to apply directly with an academic department in a school you're considering.

It's also important to know that you don't have to always speak another language fluently in order to study internationally. About 75% of American students who choose to study outside the U.S. are doing so within English-speaking countries, like Australia, Canada and the United Kingdom. Also gaining in popularity: studying in China, India, Malaysia and the United Arab Emirates.

3. Get a Tuition Discount — or Negotiate a Larger One

If you decide against foreign studies, there's no reason you can't slash domestic tuition costs by being savvy about tuition discounts.

As previously mentioned, many colleges provide tuition discounts in order to attract the applicants that they want most. The discount comes in the form of free money to cover tuition — like grants, scholarships or other merit aid from an institution that doesn't have to be repaid.

Who gets these discounts? It varies campus by campus. But generally speaking, there are four big factors that influence tuition discounting: a student's talent or academic ability; his or her ability or willingness to pay; the college's own resources; and the school's institutional priorities.

Sometimes colleges target high-achieving students, such as those with stellar grades or excellent standardized test scores, or kids who've been named National Merit Scholars. Other schools provide tuition discounts to students with special musical talent or athletic abilities. If a college or university is trying to boost its "yield," it's also more likely to offer tuition discounts and to be generous with such discounts. The number of students accepting offers of admission determines a school's yield rate. So if 1,000 students get accepted to a given college, and 30% of them enroll, then that school has a 30% yield rate.

According to a study by the National Association of College and University Business Officers (NACUBO) on tuition discounting, private schools are more likely to offer discounts than public schools. Private schools frequently discount tuition to better compete with the lower tuition "sticker price" commonly offered by public colleges and state schools. NACUBO data show that the average private school offers a 44% discount off the stated tuition rate. In fact, among private colleges studied by NACUBO, 87% of entering freshmen in the fall of 2012 received tuition discounts in the form of institutional grants or scholarships.

For standout students, "Generally speaking, the lower the quality of the school, the better the award that top students will get," says Lapovsky, who is an expert on tuition discounting.

There are two other important facts to know about tuition discounts.

First, ultra-selective schools like Harvard, Yale and Stanford are in such demand that they don't discount their tuition — even for well-off students. Ivy League schools and certain other prestigious campuses boast such strong reputations that they don't offer merit-based aid at all. Instead, these institutions only offer need-based aid to families with demonstrated financial need.

Secondly, tuition discounts are increasingly more likely to go to wealthier students than their middle-class or low-income peers. In years past, many schools offered institutional scholarships and grants to high-achieving, low-to-moderate income students who couldn't afford to pay full tuition.

These days, institutional scholarships and grants are often given to students who actually can afford to pay full tuition but aren't willing to do so. Thus, colleges use tuition discounts as a way to incentivize wealthier students to attend, knowing that those students usually have other college options.

"A student who can get into Harvard can snag a large discount from another school or is likely to get a high merit award because that school wants to improve its stats, in terms of average SAT scores and grades," Lapovsky explains.

Such discounts may have the effect of attracting students whose families can be generous donors. Discounting in this manner also becomes a revenue-producing measure to bolster tuition dollars. Look at it this way: assume a school charges $20,000 for tuition and the campus has $20,000 in grants to offer. It could offer a low-income student the full $20,000 via an institutional grant, and let that pupil attend college without worrying about tuition.

Alternatively, the school could use its $20,000 in financial aid to offer $5,000 discounts to four different wealthy kids ($5,000 x 4 = $20,000). The net result is that, with the tuition discount, each of the four rich students pays $15,000, which generates $60,000 in revenue for the school. By contrast, the low-income student — who may bring a host of other benefits, positive traits and value to the school — would nonetheless not generate tuition revenue.

This policy of discounting in favor of more affluent students — also known as financial aid leveraging — has enormous admissions implications and is controversial in many educational circles. Whether or not you agree with it, it's an increasingly common custom.

Ultimately, schools discount for two reasons: "to increase economic diversity and to shape the class that they want," Lapovsky says.

How does tuition discounting *promote* diversity in some ways, rather than diminish it? The tuition dollars generated from wealthier students often go, in part, to help support scholarships and grants that cover tuition for low-income students.

* * *

To get a tuition discount as a freshman, focus on specific types of schools:

- Private colleges rather than public colleges
- Schools that offer merit aid in addition to need-based aid
- Institutions with more financial resources and larger endowments
- Schools with lower "yield" rates
- Schools where you fit into the top 25% of the academic talent pool
- Schools where you bring something they want (a special skill, high test scores, multiculturalism, regional or socio-economic diversity, etc.)

By homing in on the latter three types of schools, you're also more likely to be admitted into the college of your choice.

Colleges employ "enrollment managers" who use all kinds of complicated formulas to determine how much of a discount to offer different types of students. One thing these enrollment specialists have found is that average-to-good students are typically more willing to enroll in schools — including high-priced institutions — even if they have to take loans out or pay more out-of-pocket to attend. Needless to say, colleges take this into account when determining tuition discounts in any given year. You should do the same.

If you get a tuition discount from an institution, you may be able to negotiate for an even larger price break than originally offered. But when you talk to a financial aid officer or an admissions counselor, don't use the word "negotiate." That rubs many school officials the wrong way. Instead, simply advise the financial aid officer that you'd like to "appeal the financial aid package based on additional information."

If you appeal an award due to your economic circumstances, let the school know about changes in your financial profile that may be significant, such as a job loss or divorce within the family.

You may also be able to subtly use another school's financial aid award letter as leverage with another school. Some students say this is particularly effective with cross-town rivals, as well as with colleges in the same general peer group, in terms of reputation and quality of the institution. Simply offer to send the letter that offers the most generous financial aid package you've received to the school you most want to attend. When you do this, let officers at your school of choice know that you'd definitely prefer to enroll there, but that their current financial offer would make it nearly impossible. Knowing this, if a school really wants you, a financial aid officer may sometimes see something in the other award letter that justifies a bigger award, or a bigger tuition discount. But there's no universal rule. Negotiating works at some colleges, and not at others.

Finally, it's also possible to use a strategy that I call "late enrollment" to get larger tuition discounts later in the admissions cycle. May 1 is known as "College Decision Day" in the world of college admissions. That's the date by which you are supposed to have evaluated your college acceptance letters and financial aid packages, and then give a deposit to a specific school, confirming that you'll be attending in the fall.

Each year, some schools don't fill all their seats as expected — meaning that fewer students than anticipated actually signed up for fall enrollment. So these schools with lower yields are actively looking for students past the May 1 deadline. The NACAC provides a list of such schools yearly, and puts out the list around the first week of May. In 2014, the NACAC list contained the names of more than 250 schools of all kinds that missed their admissions targets. Some of the schools are Baylor University, Eckerd College, Seton Hall University, Tuskegee University, University of Florida, University of Nevada Las Vegas, and the University of Vermont.

By checking this list, you can usually find colleges and universities offering steep tuition discounts. If you find a campus on the list that you've applied to, they may be willing to offer you a larger tuition discount after May 1. This strategy only works, of course, if you've not previously committed to that campus, or if you're willing to change your mind and forgo any deposit you may have paid to hold your spot at another school. You could also apply to a school on the NACAC list after May 1 in hopes of a bigger tuition discount.

Lapovsky agrees that the closer you get to the May 1 deadline, the more leverage you may have in negotiating a tuition discount. "Depending on how the school is doing, and where they are in the enrollment cycle, if enrollment is not meeting their goals, they're very likely to give you something," she says. But she suggests calling a school and trying to get that discount in April — *prior* to May 1.

As for trying to get a discount *after* May 1, it is possible, Lapovsky acknowledges, especially if you hadn't applied to the school and are just applying for the first time.

"But I'm not sure that's a strategy I would use," Lapovsky says. She explains that students who apply after May 1 "are usually students who procrastinated." Even if you had a legitimate reason for not applying earlier — for instance if you had a medical emergency — an admissions officer will still want to know why you're just getting around to applying. They may also assume that you're applying so late because every other school to which you applied turned you down.

That may or may not be the case. It could just be that none of the schools to which you were accepted offered you an affordable financial aid package. Whatever the case, be prepared to explain yourself in your application.

Summer Melt

I wouldn't advise it for the vast majority of individuals, but for a select few students who haven't applied to college but actually want to go, or for those truly needing a larger tuition discount than has been already offered, there is a final way to achieve these goals. I call this option the "summer melt" technique and it's an extreme version of the "late enrollment" strategy.

If you approach a school that is accepting applications past May 1, you may be able to use the "summer melt" strategy as a way to negotiate a better tuition discount very late in the admissions cycle, around the end of summer or early fall. Some students who've been accepted to schools on the NACAC's list can pick one of the schools around August or early September and still secure a place at the college of their choice. That's because schools dealing with "summer melt" may even try to enroll students right up until classes start. "Summer melt" occurs when students inform a school that they'll be attending in the fall, but then for some reason — a change of heart, finances, or something else — those students fail to enroll when classes begin. Such openings leave places open for students who are daring enough to try to capitalize on "summer melt."

This strategy isn't for the faint of heart. So please carefully assess the risks and only try it as a last resort. Even then, I'd suggest considering the "summer melt" strategy only if absolutely necessary. Done properly — and with some luck — you may wind up getting a much larger than usual tuition discount from a college or university you'd like to attend. However, delaying your acceptance of a school's offer could also backfire on you if you wait far too long and then find that all of a school's available slots have been taken.

4. Use the Two-Step College Option

To tackle high tuition expenses, many students start off at an affordable two-year college, earn an associate's degree, and then transfer to a four-year university where they earn their bachelor's degree. If you use this "two-step" college option, you too can drastically cut your higher education expenses since tuition at community colleges is a fraction of what you'll pay at four-year schools.

According to the College Board's Trends In College Pricing report, in the 2013-2014 academic year, tuition and fees averaged as follows among schools nationwide:

Type of School	2013-2014 Tuition and Fees
Public Two-Year In-State	$3,264
Public Four-Year In-State	$8,893
Public Four-Year Out-of-State	$22,203
Private Non-profit Four-Year	$30,094
For-Profit	$15,130

Based on those numbers alone, it may seem like a no-brainer to take the community college route when you're fresh out of high school, or you've decided to go back to school to pursue a degree.

But you do need to be aware of certain downsides and various risks associated with transferring schools.

Among the drawbacks: you won't experience immediate immersion into the campus culture at the four-year university from which you eventually hope to graduate. So it can sometimes be harder to make friends, get involved in campus clubs and activities, or just "fit in" when you're coming to a college as a junior (or in your third year) and most of your classmates have been at the school for two previous years.

Another downside: not every college will accept full college credit from every two-year campus.

A study by professors at City University of New York provides a sobering glimpse into what happens when many students move between two-year and four-year colleges. According to the study:

- Just 58% of community college transfer students were able to keep 90% or more of their credits
- 28% of transfer students lost between 11% and 90% of their credits
- The remaining 14% of community college transfer students were only able to transfer 10% or less of their credits to a four-year college.

There are other academic and financial risks inherent in being a transfer applicant.

Because most four-year colleges only have a select number of yearly slots for transfer applicants, the admissions criteria for these students is often much stricter, and grades matter more than ever. As a transfer student, all the stuff you did in high school becomes far less relevant and the academic work you did at the junior college dominates in importance over everything else. So unless you have really great grades from a community college, you may find it more difficult to transfer than you anticipated.

Additionally, transferring from one college to another can sometimes cost you more money in the long run if you don't complete your studies in four years. Unfortunately, that's often the case for students who attend multiple schools.

According to a report called "Completing College: A National View of Student Attainment Rates," conducted by the National Student Clearinghouse Research Center, only 40% of students who start at two-year public institutions obtained a bachelor's degree within a total of *six years*. By contrast, 63% of students who start their studies at four-year public colleges and 73% of students who commence their education at four-year private schools graduate in six years.

So if you do utilize the "two-step college option," you must be very strategic about this method and do some advanced planning to ensure a smooth, speedy transition.

Thankfully, there are three great ways you can do just that.

Use an Articulation Agreement

As mentioned, not being able to transfer credits can obviously hinder your ability to graduate, or graduate on time, both of which can be costly.

So before you attend any community college, find out if it has a so-called "articulation agreement" with a four year campus you'd later want to attend. Under an articulation agreement, a four-year school will guarantee that it will accept college credits from a given two-year institution. Research articulation agreements carefully and fully understand all requirements before you enroll.

It should also come as good news that certain states — among them California, Florida, Maryland, Massachusetts, Pennsylvania and Virginia — take articulation agreements one step further. Not only do they guarantee transfer of certain college credits, they also guarantee *admission* into their public four-year colleges if you complete an associate's degree at one of the state's community colleges. Such in-state partnership agreements truly help transfer students aspiring to attend four-year colleges and universities.

"Most economically strategic students I know do two years at a community college and then two years at a more prestigious school," says Lapovsky. "It's not nearly as expensive that way."

Plus, many elite schools have special articulation agreements with community colleges as part of their efforts to recruit low-income students, Lapovsky adds.

Tap Into a National Transfer Network for Community College Students

But what if you want to attend a community college and then transfer to an out-of- state school or attend a private university? In years past, there was no seamless, coordinated way to do that. But there is now.

American Honors is the only community college program in the United States that collaborates with both private and public institutions in a national network of four-year colleges and universities. Through this innovative two-year honors program, you can take virtual courses through a platform called Quad Learning, and attend classes on campus at local community colleges.

As of mid 2014, there were a half-dozen community colleges — in the states of Indiana, New Jersey and Washington — that participated in the growing American Honors network. Organizers ultimately hope to build a network of 40 to 50 community colleges, each with 500 to 1,000 students in the honors program.

Equally important, nearly three-dozen four-year colleges and universities have signed on thus far to the American Honors initiative, including some schools that offer guaranteed acceptance of transfer students who successfully complete the program.

Among the institutions in the Americans Honors network: Amherst College, Auburn University, Brandeis University, George Washington University, Middlebury College, Purdue University, Swarthmore College and Wabash College.

The American Honors program tries to distinguish itself in several ways. For starters, the coalition provides advisors to students from day one of their community college enrollment. Additionally, the honors program raises academic standards and challenges talented pupils. The goal is to immediately give high-achieving students the academic rigor as well as the tools, resources and expert advice they need to facilitate their transfer to four-year colleges.

But a chief selling point of this alliance is that it's a network that crosses state lines, and it ties into private schools too. These features allow students to broaden their list of potential four-year schools — all without worrying about the usual difficulties in transferring college credits.

Make Direct Arrangements With College Officials

If you're already at a community college, or the two-year school you're considering doesn't have an articulation agreement of any kind, you can still contact the college you wish to attend in the future and speak to an admission counselor or transfer adviser about your situation. Find out what classes would get you credit and which won't. Also ask about classes that would only meet elective requirements. Knowing a school's transfer policies ahead of time can save you a lot of time, money and frustration later.

Finally, if a two year-college won't be academically challenging enough, or if you can afford a reasonably priced four-year college, another variation on the two-step college option is to go to a state university first — for the cheaper tuition — and then matriculate to a private school that is a better fit for you, in terms of academics, social environment and other factors.

Roughly one in eight students that begin at a public or private non-profit college complete their degree at an institution different from the one where they started.

They know that in the end, it doesn't matter where you started; just where you finished. After all, it's the school you graduate from that will be the only name shown on your college diploma.

5. Go to a Fixed-price College

Hundreds of colleges and universities in America offer fixed-price tuition, a model that theoretically should save students money over four years.

If you attend a fixed-price school, the campus guarantees that the tuition rate you pay as a freshman will be the exact same rate you pay in your fourth (and hopefully final) year as a college senior.

This pricing structure could keep a bundle of money in your pocket, considering that tuition rates have generally been going up nationwide at all types of institutions.

The College Board says that tuition and fees at four-year public colleges have increased 27% in the last five years. Over the same timeframe, prices at four-year private schools increased by 14%.

You won't have to look too far to find campuses offering fixed-price tuition.

The University of Dayton has a four-year tuition model, which began in 2013-2014 and locks in the cost of tuition across a four-year period. In describing the benefits of this pricing structure, the school describes itself as follows:

"At the University of Dayton, our Catholic, Marianist mission drives us to be a catalyst for the greater good — to not just identify a problem but to take action to change it. We want students to have a successful college experience and have peace of mind regarding the cost of their degree. That's why we've created a new four-year tuition model with TOTAL TRANSPARENCY."

George Washington University also has a tuition-pricing guarantee. It's been doing it for more than a decade. Unlike many other schools, GWU locks in a set tuition price for five years, instead of just four.

Other colleges offering locked-in tuition deals include Anna Maria College in Paxton, MA; Centenary College of Louisiana in Shreveport, LA.; Concordia University in River Forest, IL; and Pace University in New York.

Starting in the 2015-2016 academic year, Ohio University will join the ranks of postsecondary schools trying to keep a lid on tuition by switching to a fixed-price tuition plan. If you keep your ears out, you'll no doubt hear of other schools doing the same.

By offering a four-year price guarantee, colleges are hoping to ease families' financial worries and help them better budget during a student's academic tenure. Schools also hope to nudge pupils along and encourage them to finish their studies on time. Better graduation rates also boost school rankings, of course, and make those institutions eligible for more federal aid. So such initiatives may not always be 100% altruistic on the part of some colleges.

Some also say there are two potential downsides to fixed-rate tuition. First, in order to spread costs out evenly over four years, colleges may front-load tuition expenses. So in the first year or two of enrollment, tuition costs can be a bit higher than anticipated. But by years three and four, students typically find that their tuition rates are lower than those for incoming freshmen.

Second, if a student drops out or transfers to another school, tuition expenses incurred in the first year or two may have been paid at a premium, without the student getting the benefit of the promised lower tuition in subsequent years.

Still, fixed-price colleges are worth consideration, especially for those who are confident about their school choice, and determined to graduate in four years.

6. Slash College Tuition by Earning a Degree in 3 Years

For some students, four years is too long to be in school — academically, socially and financially. So these students accelerate their learning and aim to finish their undergraduate studies in just three years.

If you can earn a degree in only three years, it's a major cost saver on tuition and other expenses as well.

Taking AP and CLEP exams, as well as college courses while still in high school, are sure-fire ways to push you toward earning a degree in three years. (Be sure to check out the other book in this series, *College Secrets for Teens,* for my advice on the many ways you can take standardized tests, like AP exams, for free or at a very reduced cost and save thousands on tuition).

You can zip through college faster by taking online classes in conjunction with your regular classes, taking heavier course loads during the academic year, and studying during the summer months.

It's also a good idea to target schools that specifically offer three-year programs. For example, Ball State University has a program called Degree in Three. The University of North Carolina at Greensboro has an initiative called UNCGin3, which offers priority registration to highly motivated freshman, transfer and returning students who want to complete their degrees in three years. Hartwick College in New York likewise has a three-year degree program, and Manchester University in Indiana has a program called Fast Forward that gets students out of college in three years.

Officials at the University of Charleston in Charleston, W. VA, who slashed the cost of tuition at the school by 22% a few years ago to promote affordability, are also pushing three-year degree options to save students money. At Charleston, about 25% of students earn a degree in just three years, helping to dramatically minimize debt and overall costs for those graduates.

7. Get Tuition Waivers

Tuition waivers allow you to forgo paying college tuition, or to pay greatly reduced tuition rates. Tuition waivers can offer an enormous savings for students savvy enough to track down and secure any waivers for which they qualify.

Waivers vary from college to college. But there are numerous types of waivers that are available either directly from public or private institutions, or based on benefits offered to state residents. Among the most common categories of waivers offered by schools or states are waivers for veterans, teachers, or the dependents of higher education employees.

Contessa Dickson was grateful to learn of VA benefits when her daughter enrolled at Lamar University in Beaumont, TX a couple years ago. Dickson's ex-husband had been in ROTC, and he was able to transfer his VA benefits to their daughter. She then used those military benefits to go to school at no cost.

"It paid for pretty much everything — tuition, fees, and books and supplies," Dickson said of the VA-provided college aid. "I may have spent maybe $1,000 out of pocket. Room and board would have been covered too, but my daughter lives at home."

"Some students even get VA stipends as well," Dickson added.

Check your eligibility and apply for VA benefits at: http://www.ebenefits.va.gov. You can also go online to find out if you qualify for a number of VA educational benefits.

To know exactly what waivers or benefits a school might offer, visit its website or ask campus officials directly. Usually, the Office of the Registrar handles waivers. But in some instances, the admissions office or even the financial aid office processes waivers. So it doesn't hurt to inquire at each unit.

You can also look on a state website to see the breadth of waivers available at the state level.

A good example of this strategy can be seen in the more than two dozen types of waivers offered to students attending public schools in Texas.

Some of these waivers are very unique, such as an intriguing option for entrepreneurs. Did you know that if your family owns a business and is considering relocating or expanding its offices in Texas, you can get an

Economic Development and Diversification waiver? This incentive lets employees and family members of the business pay the exact same tuition at Texas public schools that state residents pay. With this waiver, out of state students get that in-state rate even without first establishing residency, so long as the business meets certain requirements.

8. Get a Tuition Break Based on Your Parents

Wouldn't it be nice to get certain advantages in college just based on your parents' affiliations or work history? Many students know that having a parent who attended a school can give you an edge in the admissions process. If your mother or father graduated from a school you're interested in, you'd be a "legacy" student at that institution.

Beyond the admissions side of college, however, there are tuition benefits to be gained based on your parents' status.

For example, kids of academics can qualify for special tuition discounts through a nonprofit called the Tuition Exchange. It's a coalition of about 625 colleges that gives tuition breaks to the sons and daughters of college employees. You don't have to attend the school where your parent teaches or works. Your school merely has to be part of the exchange. To date, Ivy League schools aren't part of this alliance. But many excellent institutions do participate, such as Smith College, Fordham University, and the University of Southern California.

The Tuition Exchange functions through a reciprocal educational scholarship program. Schools in the exchange offer competitive scholarships to students. The scholarships cover full tuition, one-half tuition for non-residents at public schools, or offer a rate established by the Tuition Exchange. For the 2014-2015 school year, institutions whose tuition price exceeds $32,500 can award scholarships for less than their full tuition, but not less than the set rate of $32,500. In 2015-2016, the set rate is established at $33,000.

Separately, the Tuition Exchange in 2014 launched a new annual "Seat Space Availability Service."

Just like the National Association for College Admission Counseling survey, Tuition Exchange now polls its member schools yearly to see which institutions will still accept applications for fall enrollment after the May 1 college response deadline.

As of early May 2014, there were 84 Tuition Exchange member colleges able to offer at least 510 seats to freshmen or transfer students. So seeking entry to one of these schools could net you an even larger tuition discount. The Tuition Exchange will maintain its list of colleges with available space through mid-August of each year.

Get Legacy Tuition Benefits and Scholarships

A slew of other schools also offer legacy tuition benefits and scholarships to children of alumni, helping to slash higher education costs.

Here's a sampling of these tuition savers at colleges and universities nationwide.

The University of Kentucky offers a Legacy Tuition Program that grants partial tuition awards to eligible non-residents who are children of UK graduates.

At Pittsburgh State University, a Legacy Program helps students save about $7,500 by shaving out-of-state tuition expenses.

Kansas University has a Jayhawks Generation Scholarship Program that gives lucrative tuition discounts to out-of-state freshman whose parents or grandparents graduated from the university. The discounts can equal nearly $50,000 over four years — a massive savings for good students who qualify.

Southern Illinois University has a Legacy Alternate Tuition Rate for entering freshman or transfer undergraduates whose parents or legal guardians are graduates. Under the program, eligible students pay a tuition rate of just 0.80 times the applicable in-state or out-of state cost of tuition.

9. Take Advantage of In-state Bargains

One of the most obvious ways to reduce your tuition costs is to go to an in-state school, where tuition and fees are much lower than what you'd pay at an out-of-state college.

On average, in-state residents are charged one-third to one-half of the tuition that non-residents are charged for tuition.

One campus with relatively modest in-state tuition is the University of Delaware.

That's where Chrissi Lockwood was very happy to see her daughter, Kati, go off to school as a freshman in the 2013-2014 school year. Resident tuition at the university was $10,580 for the term.

"She got a scholarship for playing the oboe in the marching band, and it covered nearly all of her tuition," Lockwood said of her daughter's $10,000 scholarship.

Kati also received a $400 stipend for being in the school's pep band. "It's not a huge amount of money, but it definitely helps with her spending money," Lockwood says.

Best of all, Lockwood's daughter is close enough to family, yet far enough away to have her own life as she navigates college issues and plans for her graduation in 2017.

"Kati loves the University of Delaware," Lockwood says. "She's extremely busy because she's a dual degree student earning a B.A. in music and a B.S. in science, in food science. She also made the Dean's list in the first semester for both schools."

Proud parents like Lockwood are often coming to the U.S. from other nations too, hoping to give their children a quality education — as well as a chance at a better future.

Increasingly, students originally born in other countries — including many undocumented immigrants — can qualify for resident or in-state tuition.

In May 2014, Florida became the 20th state in the nation to grant in-state tuition rates to students brought to the U.S. illegally as minors.

There are roughly 65,000 undocumented students living in the U.S. who graduate each year from high school. Of those pupils, between 5% and 10% of them attend college, estimates from the American Association of State Colleges and Universities show.

So if you happen to be one of those students, know that you can take advantage of in-state tuition now offered in many states in America. For the latest info on this trend, check the website of The National Conference of State Legislatures, which tracks the topic of tuition for undocumented students.

10. Take Courses in the Summer

Many colleges lower their tuition rates for students taking summer classes. It's easy to understand their rationale. Dorms are empty — or at least nowhere near capacity. Most faculty members are away, and many school programs and services simply aren't operating at full throttle in June, July or early August.

Thus, summer students can bring in additional revenue for a campus during what's traditionally the slow part of the academic year.

So if you're willing to study when your classmates might be working, doing internships or just goofing off at the beach, you can save money on higher education costs.

The University of Texas at Austin has a tuition discount policy in force for students who enroll in summer courses. Tuition for these summer classes is 15% less than classes taken during the fall or spring terms.

11. Pre-pay for Tuition to Save Money

At scores of institutions nationwide, students and their families have a chance to save thousands of dollars on future tuition expenses by prepaying based on today's tuition price.

The sooner you pay, the more you can save.

For those who are able to pre-pay for college expenses, they typically save about 10% off their college bills for each year's worth of expenses covered.

Even if your school of choice doesn't offer its own direct pre-paid tuition option, you should look into whether the college is listed as part of a group called Private College 529. This organization, to which more than 270 private schools belong, lets families sock away as little as $25 to start a 529 college savings account and they can make additional pre-payments of just $25. Obviously, if you take this route, you should try to save more. But those figures just show you how little you can set aside and still take advantage of a tuition pre-payment method.

When you save money through Private College 529, you get tuition certificates that you can use at any one of the member colleges. You must save for at least three years to later use those certificates. But since the certificates are portable, you don't have to lock in or choose any particular school upfront.

The Private College 529 Plan is established and maintained by Tuition Plan Consortium, LLC, a non-profit organization. OFI Private Investments Inc., a subsidiary of Oppenheimer Funds, Inc., manages the program. (Be sure to see *College Secrets for Teens* for details on the benefits of 529 plans, as well as my tips for the best ways to save for college).

12. Tap Into Pipeline and Pathway Programs

Pipeline programs are designed to promote college readiness and college access for underrepresented students in a variety of fields. Many colleges have pipeline programs designed for both high schools students, and middle school students too. The idea is to give targeted individuals — such as low-income youth, minorities, first-generation college students and others — as early an introduction as possible to a given academic discipline or industry. Pipeline programs are particularly common in STEM areas, or Science, Technology, Engineering and Math.

Besides promoting college preparedness and access, pipeline programs frequently provide a pathway to a more affordable higher education as well.

That's because students who successfully complete pipeline programs are often offered free or discounted tuition at selected colleges and universities.

One highly successful initiative is the Future Scholars Program at Rutgers University, which currently serves a total of about 1,000 youth. It's a completely free, 5-year pre-college program. Academically ambitious, low-income students apply for the program during 7th grade. After being accepted, students receive an array of benefits from 8th grade through their senior year of high school:

- Participants attend free summer programs, including residential experiences
- They hone their skills in reading, writing, math, physics and chemistry
- Students attend college information workshops on campus
- They get individualized tutoring for their most challenging subjects
- Students receive coaching to perform well on college admissions tests

Best of all, Rutgers grants full tuition scholarships to students who successfully complete the program and are later admitted to the school.

That's a terrific deal any way you look at it. Even if a student chooses *not* to apply to Rutgers, because an application isn't a requirement of the program, the Future Scholars Program still prepares youth for any college of their dreams — as well as other pursuits.

"We take 200 students every year and provide them with the academic, social, emotional and financial support to help them succeed," says Aramis Gutierrez, Program Director of the Rutgers Future Scholars Program.

"Our main goal is to ensure that students find the right fit for them — whether that's here at Rutgers, at another four-year institution, a two-year college, or even doing something else," he adds, noting: "We guide them accordingly, regardless of whether or not they pursue college, because some students are interested in working after high school, or engaging in community service, or even joining the military."

International students should know that just as there are pipeline programs for under-represented minorities and others, there are likewise "pathway" programs for international students.

Inside Higher Education has chronicled several pathway programs for foreign students who study in the U.S. While these offerings vary greatly by institution, a key benefit is that many of these programs ultimately save students money on tuition.

How is this done? In essence, pathway programs for international students work by accelerating a student's undergraduate work and helping the student more seamlessly transition through the American higher education system.

Instead of spending time and money improving their English through an intensive ESL program, a student gets to combine English and academic study right away, and immediately start amassing credits toward his or her four-year degree.

13. Attend a Work College

There are seven federally recognized "work colleges" in America where students can earn while they learn. If you get into one of these colleges, you'll be happy that your tuition is either free or very low compared to the vast majority of U.S. colleges and universities.

Work colleges have been around for over 150 years. But they're growing even more popular as students grapple with rising tuition and other exploding higher education expenses.

The seven work colleges you should be familiar with are: Alice Lloyd College in Pippa Passes, KY; Berea College in Berea, KY; Blackburn College in Carlinville, IL; College of the Ozarks in Point Lookout, MO; Ecclesia College in Springdale, Arkansas, Sterling College in Craftsbury Common, VT; and Warren Wilson College in Swannanoa, NC.

A few highlights of some of these colleges:

Alice Lloyd, Berea, and College of the Ozarks don't charge students tuition. The other work colleges offer low-to-moderately priced tuition and other financial aid.

All students at Alice Lloyd College are required to work at least 10 hours per week in exchange for free tuition. If students need additional aid to cover room and board, they can work up to 20 hours per week. Jobs are assigned based on a student's own preferences and prior work experience.

College of the Ozarks requires students to work 15 hours a week plus two 40-hour workweeks during the year. The school provides all students with full-tuition scholarships and grants. Each year, College of the Ozarks receives about 4,000 applications and admits roughly 300 to 350 students for the fall term. The school also routinely has a waiting list of students vying to be accepted. Applicants are chosen on the basis of financial need, academics, leadership, and service.

While 71% of all U.S. college grads wind up with debt, only half of those who attend work colleges have student debt upon graduation. And when they do, it's usually about one-third to one-half of what their peers at other institutions have.

According to the Work Colleges Consortium, school programs vary from campus to campus. But they all have several things in common. For starters, work colleges mandate that in exchange for free or reduced tuition, students must engage in labor activity, usually between 10 and 15 hours of work per week. These programs also teach students the importance of service, as well as leadership skills and the ability to juggle multiple priorities, such as school and work.

"No students can buy their way out of the work program. That is not an option. So the work levels the playing field," says Robin Taffler, Executive Director of the Work Colleges Consortium.

According to Taffler, students at work colleges run all the schools' institutional functions.

"Students do gardening on school grounds, they run the IT desk, handle electrical work and plumbing repairs, and they even build all the buildings at the College of the Ozarks," Taffler said.

"They're trained firefighters," she adds. "They do billing and accounts payable. They work in the President's office. They do research and organize events. At Berea College, students manage the forests, they take care of livestock and work in the cafeteria and manage food services. Students at work colleges literally do everything."

Because work itself is core to the schools' philosophy, it is also integrated into the academic structure. There are Deans of Work, students get evaluated on their work, and students can even be kicked out of work colleges if their work is not up to snuff.

"It's very different from federal work study, which is an optional, need-based program," Taffler notes.

"At Work Colleges, 100% of our students work for all 4 years. They graduate with real work experience," Taffler says. "They are sought-after by employers because they know how to show up for work, they have basic workplace skills, as well as more advanced, sophisticated skills in various areas."

Can You Really Just Work To Put Yourself Through College?

If you're one of the vast majority of U.S. students who doesn't attend a work college, you can nonetheless work while you're in school, on your own or through a "work study" program offered by the U.S. Department of Education. Students who use federal "work study" have jobs either on campus or off campus. The money earned can be used as a credit to reduce tuition expenses or to pay other college costs.

But since Work Colleges are either tuition-free or charge very low tuition rates, they provide a more realistic opportunity to graduate debt-free in a way that isn't usually possible for students working while attending other institutions.

That's because if you're attending a typical four-year public or private college where the tuition is within average levels — anywhere from $8,000 to $30,000+ annually — then you'll probably never realistically earn enough to cover all your school costs.

Among four-year public schools, the average price of tuition rose 2.9% in 2013-2014. That was actually the smallest tuition increase in nearly 30 years. For many years prior to 2013, the price of tuition surged anywhere from 5% to 10% annually.

These are economic realities that parents, grandparents and other adults need to be sensitive to in today's college environment.

It's easy for those who earned a degree a generation ago (or longer) to say something like: "When I was in college, I worked my way through school and I paid for everything myself." Others will even add statements like: "I don't understand students today. I didn't take out student loans, and I didn't ask my parents or the government for money, either."

Well, it was possible 25 or more years ago to work your way through school, based on wages back then and the relatively reasonable college costs of a generation ago. But college costs have skyrocketed over the past two-plus decades and wages have not kept pace. That scenario has effectively made higher education unaffordable even for most adults who are working full time. Certainly, teens or young adults who are studying full time don't have the earnings power to foot the bill for all of their school costs.

* * *

Randy Olson, a graduate student at Michigan State University, wanted to investigate the issue of whether it was possible for a student at Michigan State to work in order to put him or herself through school.

Olson's findings were as follows:

"What we see is a startling trend: Modern students have to work as much as 6x longer to pay for college than 30 years ago. Given the reports that a growing number of college students are working minimum wage jobs, this spells serious trouble for any student who hopes to work their way through college without any additional support."

Olson concludes: *"Perhaps it's no surprise that tuition costs are rising, and college is becoming less and less affordable by the year. Yet somehow, the idea that we can work our way through college still persists. This ethos seems to be the latest generation's version of the American Dream: If you work long and hard enough, and if you sacrifice enough, you will eventually graduate college without debt and land your dream job. But with the way this trend is going, it looks like even long and hard hours at work won't even pay off any more.*

In short, I'd like my readers to walk away knowing that it's not nearly as easy to work your way through college as it used to be — stop telling us to do it just because you did a decade or more ago."

Interestingly, Olson later went on to examine what was happening nationally — not just at his campus.

His later findings echoed his earlier research — demonstrating that it's simply *not possible* for most students to use work alone as a way to put themselves through college.

In summary, Olson found that nationwide, the average university student in 1979 only had to work 182 hours per year to pay for tuition. That's the equivalent of having a part-time summer job. By contrast, the average college student in 2013 had to work a whopping 991 hours to cover tuition. That's the same as holding down a full-time job for half of the year.

As Olson points out, the disparity in work hours is huge: modern students must work more than five times as many hours just to get the same education as their predecessors did back in 1979.

It's worth noting that Olson's data only refers to *public* school tuition for *in-state residents*. We all know that private school costs a lot more, as does tuition for out-of-state residents. Furthermore, as you've learned thus far, tuition is just *one* of many higher education costs. Even if a student could earn enough to cover tuition that wouldn't pay for room and board, books and supplies and other necessities.

So parents and others, encourage your kids to work if you want. But do cut students some slack when it comes to the outdated notion of working one's way through college absent any other financial support.

14. Have Your Employer Pay

According to a survey by Citigroup and *Seventeen* magazine, nearly four out of five U.S. students work while in school. That includes students in high schools, community colleges, online institutions, and four-year colleges and universities. The average working student logs 19 hours a week during the academic year, the study found.

Many students work in order to have spending money, not necessarily to cover upfront school expenses like tuition. In fact, the Citigroup study found that even after working nearly 20 hours a week, only a fraction of employed students paid their own tuition: 41% of students indicated that they rely on financial aid; 22% of students said their parents pay; only 18% reported that they pay their own way; and 16% said they had scholarships to cover tuition.

If you are among those students who work part-time, or even full time, you may have a ready option to cut your tuition expense: simply ask your employer to pay it or to reimburse you for this cost.

The Compdata Surveys Benefits USA survey of 4,500 companies found that 76% of firms in America offer tuition reimbursement to *some* employees. Additionally, 57% of businesses now offer reimbursement to *all* employees. That's up dramatically from the 35% of companies that offered this benefit to all workers back in 2009. The good news about this growing trend is that more people, even *part-time* workers, can secure tuition help.

Employer subsidies for tuition vary by industry, but reimbursements often fall within the $3,000 to $5,000 range annually. Some employers, though, are far more generous with tuition assistance. Compdata says that 25% of companies place no limit at all on the amount that an employee can be reimbursed for tuition.

In today's competitive marketplace, employers offer tuition assistance as a way to attract employees, reward them, and retain top talent. So don't be afraid to inquire of your boss or human resources specialist about this potential company perk. When you do, ask about any tuition reimbursement limits, as well as minimum grade or post-reimbursement work requirements that your company may impose.

15. Work in a High-Need Field Where the College Will Pay Your Tuition

It takes employees of all kinds to work in a variety of jobs that improve local communities and the wellbeing of residents who live there.

Depending on your college major and intended career path, you may be able to work in an area that has a shortage of needed professionals and work specialists. These areas are known as "high need fields" and colleges will often pay you to study and work in these areas because they know you'll ultimately be helping society at large.

For example, the University of Portland has a special nursing initiative called the Providence Scholars Program, under which the school will pay most of your tuition for two years if you agree to work in certain areas after you graduate from college. The tuition aid comes partially from the university, but mostly from Oregon Providence Health & Services, which has partnered with the school for this effort.

Schools aren't the only entities that offer paid tuition for those entering high-need fields. Similar opportunities exist via national groups such as Teach for America, the National Institutes of Health, and the Nursing Education Loan Repayment Program.

So if you plan on having a career in health, medicine, education or other areas where there's a shortage of trained professionals, do look into campus-based or organizational programs that will offer to pay your tuition in whole or in part.

16. Find a College With a Tuition Guarantee Program

Tuition guarantee programs represent another smart way to cut your tuition expenses. Don't confuse a tuition guarantee program with a fixed-priced tuition offering. They're different. Fixed-rate schools, as previously mentioned, promise that they'll lock in a specific rate of tuition over four or five years.

With a tuition guarantee program, however, a college or university promises to pay your tuition if you don't graduate in four years.

One such program is Temple University's new "Fly in 4" initiative, which launched in the 2014-2015 school year. Under the "Fly in 4" program, Temple limits the number of hours per week that students have to work, and the school guarantees that students can still graduate in four years. Temple reduces the workload of 500 students annually by giving those with financial need annual grants of $4,000. These funds allow students to devote more time to studying and less time to working.

But the "Fly in 4" Program doesn't go one-way. Students must also meet certain obligations, such as consulting each semester with an academic advisor, registering early for classes, and completing a graduation review at or prior to completing 90 credits.

If, for some reason, students still can't graduate on time, but they've fulfilled all of their responsibilities, Temple will pick up the tuition cost of any remaining classes.

That's a sweet deal for diligent students who take their academics seriously but need financial assistance to avoid working too much. Incoming freshman and transfer applicants are eligible for the program.

The Fly in 4 initiative is the brainchild of Temple's president, Neil D. Theobald, who came to the university in 2013. An expert in higher education finance, Theobald was the first in his family to go to college, which was made possible because he got a full scholarship.

As a result of his own personal and professional experiences — Theobald was also the former Chief Financial Officer at Indiana University — he has made college affordability and lowering student debt a priority at Temple.

"What we've found is that students from low- and middle-income backgrounds tend to take longer to complete their degrees, in part because they spend a lot of time working," Theobald said in announcing the Fly in 4 Program.

But for nearly 50 years, "researchers have shown that college students employed more than 15 hours per week during the school year earn much lower grades than do those working fewer hours for pay," Theobald said. "In addition, time-to-graduation has become the primary determinant of student debt."

"Temple students must not keep their futures waiting," Theobald added. "Under this initiative, our students will be able to limit their debt and advance more quickly into careers that will allow them to pay off the debt they do acquire."

There are other benefits from tuition guarantee programs as well.

For the state of Texas, a legislative initiative rewards students who graduate on time. It's called the Texas BOT, or the "B-On-Time Loan Repayment" program and it offers low-interest loans to financially needy students who start out at two-year community colleges and four-year public colleges, as well as private universities. And here's the kicker: those college loans are later forgiven for undergraduates who finish their studies within specified time limits. Furthermore, undergrads can receive tuition rebates of up to $1,000 if they graduate on schedule.

You now know 16 ways to drastically reduce any tuition bill you may face. But these aren't the only tuition-busting methods at your disposal. Let's turn now to what you can do to reduce tuition if you happen to attend college out of state.

$\mathcal{T}$UITION $\mathcal{T}$RICKS FOR OUT-OF-$\mathcal{S}$TATE $\mathcal{S}$TUDENTS

Going to school out of state presents additional obstacles for students and their families. You might get homesick a lot — especially in the beginning. You have higher travel costs and more logistics to handle when you want to get back home for the holidays or during the summer.

But one of the biggest hurdles associated with attending college out of state is a financial one: many schools charge much higher tuition rates for non-residents than in-state residents. The differences in tuition can sometimes be enormous.

Let's look, for example, at tuition costs in public schools in three states: California, Florida and Texas.

Why these regions? It's because they generate a boatload of college-bound students.

Did you know that these three states alone — California, Florida, and Texas — produce about half of the country's 3.3 million high school graduates?

So let's examine in-state and out-of-state tuition and fees at UCLA, Florida State University, and the University of Texas at Austin.

College/ University	2014-2015 In-State Tuition & Fees	2014-2015 Out-of-State Tuition & Fees
Univ. of California, Los Angeles	$14,800	$35,740
Florida State University	$6,592	$22,494
University of Texas, Austin	$10,052	$34,722

As you can see, out-of-state students attending these schools are charged tuition rates totaling roughly 2.5 to 3.5 times the rate charged to their in-state classmates.

I know it may not seem fair. But one of the realities of higher education today — at least among public colleges and universities — is that these schools are getting less money from state and federal sources. As a result, they are increasingly looking to out-of-state students, along with international students, to make up the difference. Colleges and universities do that by charging non-residents a surcharge on tuition. For many families, these enormous tuition surcharges can be cost-prohibitive.

The College Board reports that in the 2013-2014 school term, out-of-state students nationwide were charged an average of just over $13,000 more in tuition than their in-state peers.

The numbers can seem daunting. But don't despair if you're set on attending or are already attending an out-of-state college or university.

In addition to the tuition reduction strategies outlined in the previous chapter, there are some additional techniques you can use to shave tuition expenses.

Here are eight ways to lower tuition costs when you're an out-of-state student:

1. Use a regional student exchange program
2. Ask for a border waiver
3. Get a non-resident tuition waiver
4. Consider moving
5. Go to a flat-tuition school
6. Get institutional scholarships
7. Use your public service benefits
8. Get tuition waivers for special circumstances

1. Use a Regional Student Exchange Program

About one out of five freshmen attending public four-year colleges and universities study out of state, according to the National Center for Education Statistics. Fortunately, many states have reciprocity agreements with neighboring states that allow students to pay less than the published tuition prices for non-residents.

These reciprocity agreements are also known as regional student exchange programs.

You've probably heard of exchange programs where students attend school in different countries.

Well, there are also domestic exchange programs of a sort.

In order to advance higher education, some states share educational resources with one another and their residents. They do this by joining an interstate coalition (known as a "compact") and then facilitating regional student exchange programs.

Although each interstate compact has its own nuances, in general, member states allow residents of nearby states to get specified tuition discounts. A student must usually also study a major that is not available in his or her own home state.

So the state of Florida, for instance, might allow Georgia residents to attend the University of Florida for the same tuition price charged to Florida locals. That would amount to many thousands in savings annually.

Other states let out-of-towners pay no more than 1.5 or 1.75 times the rate that residents pay.

In addition to the obvious money-saving benefits, regional exchange programs boast a lot of other good features. One advantage: you don't have to meet any specific income or financial aid requirements to get the tuition discounts afforded by regional exchange programs. In most cases, you don't even have to fill out the FAFSA (although I recommend that you do always complete the FAFSA, for reasons I'll explain later in Chapter 9 of this book).

Here are seven large regional student-exchange programs that let you get in-state tuition, or greatly reduced tuition, even if you reside out of state. These tuition breaks are offered primarily at public schools, but also at private institutions where noted.

New England Region

The New England Regional Student Program (RSP) is open to residents of six states: Connecticut, Maine, Massachusetts, New Hampshire, Rhode Island and Vermont.

Public colleges and universities in these states agree that non-residents from the region will not pay more than 1.75 times a school's in-state tuition rate. Eligible students must study a major not available in their home state. Under this program, participating New England students save roughly $7,000 a year in tuition. More than 750 associate, bachelor's and graduate degree programs are offered and the initiative, dubbed "RSP Tuition Break," is available at all 82 of New England's public colleges and universities.

The New England Board of Higher Education (NEBHE) governs the six member states of the New England Regional Student Program. NEBHE's website has a "find a program" section and state-specific brochures detailing the exact programs of study available at each institution.

Midwestern Region

The Midwest Student Exchange is open to students in nine states: Illinois, Indiana, Kansas, Michigan, Minnesota, Missouri, North Dakota, Nebraska, and Wisconsin.

More than 100 colleges and universities participate in this exchange program. These schools agree that non-residents from the region will not pay more than 1.5 times the in-state resident tuition rate for specific programs. Participating students can save up to $5,000 annually. Private colleges and universities also offer a 10% tuition discount.

The Midwestern Higher Education Compact (MHEC) governs the Midwest Student Exchange. Although 12 Midwestern states belong to this compact, the Midwest Student Exchange program is voluntary, and only nine states participate. Currently, residents of Iowa, Ohio and South Dakota aren't eligible to take part in the exchange.

Since participating states and programs can change, however, make sure you visit the website for the latest details on each program.

Western Region

The Western Undergraduate Exchange is open to students in 15 states: Alaska, Arizona, California, Colorado, Hawaii, Idaho, Montana, Nevada, New Mexico, North Dakota, Oregon, South Dakota, Utah, Washington and Wyoming.

The exchange is also open to students in six other regions: the three U.S. Pacific Territories (American Samoa, the Commonwealth of the

Northern Mariana Islands, and Guam); and the three Freely Associated States, (the Federated States of Micronesia, the Marshall Islands, and Palau). Collectively, these territories are deemed as the 16th member of the Western Undergraduate Exchange.

Under this program, out-of-state students pay tuition that is capped at 1.5 times resident tuition. More than 150 public two-year and four-year institutions in the region participate. Savings vary per campus, but average about $7,500 per student. Since the number of eligible students is limited to about 36,000 individuals each year, it's best to apply as early as possible.

The Western Regional Graduate Program is another exchange for graduate students in the 16 aforementioned Western states and territories. There are 56 participating universities offering roughly 320 graduate programs to non-resident students at in-state tuition rates. In 2013-2014, the average student pursuing a master's degree, graduate certificate or a PhD saved about $14,000 through this program.

The Professional Student Exchange Program (PSEP) is a discounted tuition program to students enrolled in 10 specific healthcare programs in 12 member states: Alaska, Arizona, Colorado, Hawaii, Idaho, Montana, Nevada, New Mexico, North Dakota, Utah, Washington, Wyoming. This exchange program is not currently available to students in three Western states: California, Oregon, and South Dakota.

PSEP covers professional degrees in dentistry, allopathic medicine, osteopathic medicine, physician assistant, physical therapy, occupational therapy, optometry, pharmacy, podiatry, and veterinary medicine.

Under this exchange program, out-of-state students attending public institutions pay in-state tuition rates or reduced tuition. Those attending private schools also get tuition breaks. Moreover, PSEP students can receive "support payments" to help cover their tuition. These support payments are paid directly to a student's school. Funds vary by professional area of study, but the 2014-2015 support fee rate ranged from $7,400 to $31,500.

The Western Interstate Commission for Higher Education (WICHE) governs the Western Undergraduate Exchange, the Western Regional Graduate Program, as well as the Professional Student Exchange Program.

In the 2013-2014 school year, WICHE's three exchange programs saved more than 35,600 undergraduate, graduate and professional students $265 million in tuition.

Southern Region

The Academic Common Market is open to students in 16 states: Alabama, Arkansas, Delaware, Florida, Georgia, Kentucky, Louisiana, Maryland, Mississippi, North Carolina, Oklahoma, South Carolina, Tennessee, Texas, Virginia, and West Virginia.

Under this exchange program, individuals studying in specialized fields at out-of-state colleges pay in-state tuition rates — provided they pursue degrees in areas not offered by their home state's institutions. More than 100 colleges and universities participate in the Academic Common Market and more than 1,900 undergraduate and graduate degree programs are available.

The Regional Contract Program, which aids graduate students in the healthcare area, is open to residents in eight Southern states: Arkansas, Delaware, Georgia, Kentucky, Louisiana, Mississippi, South Carolina, and Tennessee. Residents of the other eight Southern states — Alabama, Florida, Maryland, North Carolina, Oklahoma, Texas, Virginia and West Virginia — are not currently eligible to participate in the Regional Contract Program.

Under this program, students seeking professional health degrees at out-of-state institutions pay in-state tuition at public colleges and universities, or reduced tuition at private institutions.

The South Regional Education Board is responsible for the Academic Common Market and the Regional Contract Program.

* * *

Since policies governing regional exchange programs vary from state to state, and from school to school, it's best to ask your college or university for its specific requirements and deadlines. Also, to take full advantage of a tuition reciprocity agreement, be prepared to apply for your tuition break well in advance of when you'll need it; application processing times can sometimes run several months.

Unfortunately, three states in the U.S. — New Jersey, New York and Pennsylvania — do not belong to any regional compact. So students in those states can't participate in one of these regional exchanges.

You may have also noticed that one other state, North Dakota, actually belongs to more than one compact. That means residents in this state have a wider array of options when it comes to picking out-of-state schools and still getting in-state or reduced tuition.

As a final note, for those interested in online or distance learning, know that many regional exchanges offer tuition reductions and other support through those educational options as well.

2. Get a Border Waiver

Obtaining a "border waiver" is another way to slash tuition for non-resident students.

In addition to the regional exchanges and interstate compacts previously described, some states and schools have their own direct tuition reciprocity agreements with border states or specific schools. Under these direct agreements, you can obtain a border waiver from a school, allowing you to take advantage of in-state tuition.

A case in point is the University of Utah, which has a Border Waiver Program for non-resident students from certain high schools located near the border of Utah.

The school's waiver initiative lowers the annual tuition rate for out-of-state students to 1.5 times the resident tuition. The program spells out eligible high schools — in three Wyoming cities, as well as one city in Nevada — whose students are eligible to receive the tuition reduction.

The University of Utah gives out 27 border awards each year, and they're awarded on a first-come, first-served basis.

Like many schools, Utah grants priority status for waivers to entering freshman students. But when waivers are available, transfer students and graduate students may be eligible as well.

If you'll be an out of town student, do an Internet search of the term "border waiver" along with the name of the college you want to attend. You'll find that some schools even have direct border waiver agreements with specific counties, and even Canada, as do the states of Minnesota and North Dakota, permitting drastic tuition reductions for non-residents.

3. Get a Non-resident Tuition Waiver

A non-resident tuition waiver grants you a special exemption from paying out of state tuition rates. With this waiver, a student who isn't a legal resident of the state nonetheless pays in-state tuition. In certain cases, when a non-resident waiver is granted, schools require non-residents to pay resident tuition cost, plus a small surcharge. But that surcharge is always a fraction of what you'd normally pay in out-of-state tuition expenses.

One example of an institution that offers the latter type of program is Clark College, which provides non-resident waivers to U.S. citizens, permanent residents and refugees who have recently moved to the state of Washington. Clark is quite generous in allowing non-residents to readily qualify for its tuition reduction program.

According to the school's website, an in-state resident is a person who meets the qualifications of citizenship mentioned above and who has been domiciled in the state of Washington for a minimum of 12 months prior to the beginning of the quarter.

However, those who meet the qualifications of citizenship listed above, but have been domiciled in the state of Washington for *less* than 12 months prior to the beginning of the quarter can still receive the non-resident tuition waiver.

In fact, you could live in Washington for less than a week and still qualify for this amazing tuition break.

Clark College states that "students who do not meet the legal definition of a Washington resident will qualify for this waiver as long as they are domiciled in the state of Washington *by the first day* [my emphasis added] of the term they plan to enroll. This waiver is available to U.S. citizens, permanent resident aliens, or eligible non-immigrant aliens with visa classifications A, E, G, I or K."

To prove that you have moved to Washington and established domicile, you need only fill out Clark's application for non-resident waiver, and supply at least one of the following pieces of evidence showing your new residency in the state of Washington:

- a rental or lease agreement
- a closing statement of a home purchase

- a Washington driver's license
- a vehicle registration
- a voter's identification card

Furthermore, after students have established Washington residency for at least 12 months, they can submit a Residency Reclassification application and appropriate documentation in order to be considered for in-state tuition rates at Clark College.

Clark certainly isn't alone.

Colleges and universities of all kinds offer these tuition waivers. A quick online search of the phrase "non-resident tuition waiver" or "non-resident waiver," along with the name of your desired school, will let you know what might be available.

Even if you don't see anything on the school's website, you can still research whether the state in which the college or university is located has any special laws affording tuition waivers to specific types of students.

* * *

One good way to find schools that have nixed out-of-state tuition and bucked the trend of charging non-resident tuition, is to seek out institutions and states with aggressive recruitment efforts underway.

One such major recruitment drive is currently taking place in Mississippi, where post secondary schools rely heavily on tuition but have largely struggled to attract students.

State funding for Mississippi colleges has stagnated in recent years and schools there have faced tough competition from other regional institutions, such as the University of South Alabama, which waived non-resident fees for Mississippi residents.

So in 2012, Mississippi state legislators passed a law allowing colleges and universities to reduce tuition to in-state levels for out-of-state students in a bid to increase enrollment and entice non-resident students who otherwise wouldn't attend. After getting state approval, Delta State University became the first of Mississippi's eight public universities to allow all non-Mississippi residents to pay the same tuition rates as students who live in the state.

Delta's tuition waivers for all out of state students went into effect in the fall of 2013, and most other Mississippi state schools quickly followed suit. Non-residents save about $6,000 to $10,000 annually because of the change.

For its part, Ole Miss — the University of Mississippi — isn't taking part in the same wholesale recruitment initiative that grants tuition waivers to all out-of-state students, according to Admissions Director Whitman Smith.

Smith says the University of Mississippi is fortunate enough to already have "an extremely healthy interest out of state" thanks to the great value the school offers and its abundance of academic programs and extracurricular opportunities for studies. Whitman notes that out-of-state tuition at the campus is currently around $19,000, one of the lowest amounts in the country for a flagship state school.

As a result, "40% of our students are typically from out of state, and over the last three years more than 50% of our student body has been from outside Mississippi," Whitman says.

It's a trend he expects to continue, especially as some states grapple with more student demand to access higher education, as well as admissions policies that favor in-state residents.

"This year, in terms of applicants, one of our largest states is California. For students there, it's very hard to get in (to California state schools), and if you do get in, it's increasingly difficult to pay for it. Then if you can pay for it, it's still hard to get the courses you need" because of class size, Whitman says.

He's seeing the same trend from other states too. In particular, Whitman says more students are seeking admission to Ole Miss from the state of Texas — where public colleges automatically accept the top 10%, or in the case of UT Austin, the top 8% of in-state students — and applications are up from Georgia too, where students compete for HOPE scholarships.

Unlike its peer schools within the state that have begun to offer tuition waivers to all out-of-state students who are admitted, Smith says the University of Mississippi offers selective out-of-state tuition waivers and scholarships to specific students, including military veterans, academically talented freshmen with high grades and test scores, students enrolling in

STEM programs, as well as students from specific geographic regions that Ole Miss wants to target.

"We're extremely aware of the rising cost of college and we do as much as we can to help students," Smith says.

4. Consider Moving for Lower Tuition

To take advantage of in-state tuition, some students take the drastic step of moving to the state in which their desired college or university is located. When this strategy works, it can save you tens of thousands of dollars. But be forewarned: it's not as easy as you might think.

Over the past decade or so, many schools have tightened up their residency policies and gotten much stricter about who qualifies for in-state tuition. Although a lot of schools may be fairly lenient about this matter, generally speaking, that's not the case with top-tier public schools and in-demand private schools that charge out-of-state tuition to non-residents.

If you or your family are considering moving — perhaps for a parent's job, but also to score a low-rate tuition deal — there are three main questions you need to ask and get answered from the school of your choice.

1. What is the precise definition of a resident, as well as a non-resident for tuition purposes?
2. What documentation is required to prove residency?
3. Are non-resident tuition waivers available, and if so what is the eligibility criteria to receive them?

If you're a dependent student, realize that it's not enough for you to move on your own. You must typically have at least one parent also move to the state where your school is located. That parent usually has to have resided in the state for a year or more before you enroll in college, in order for you to get resident tuition.

Rules vary across the country; the residency requirement is only six months in Arkansas, but it's 24 months in Alaska. Tennessee has no specific length of time that it mandates for residency. As mentioned earlier, in the case of Clark College, certain schools can offer non-resident tuition waivers that give the exact same benefits you'd get by moving and becoming an in-state resident.

* * *

But some institutions may deny you resident tuition if it seems you only recently relocated, or that you did so for the sole purpose of getting a break on tuition.

For the best possible chance at proving residency, plan on showing documentation that proves you (and a parent) moved to the state at least a year or more prior to your initial enrollment date.

The documentation can be anything that demonstrates that you have established legal domicile or that you intend to maintain permanent residency, and aren't merely a temporary resident. So a home purchase, rental agreements or housing lease may aid you — particularly if you can show that you've been living in the residence, not just using it as a second home or vacation property. Doing other things like voting, filing a state tax return in the new state, or transferring your car registration from your old state to the new one will also bolster your case. Just having serious social, civic or professional ties in the local community can help establish bona fide residency as well. All of these things can pave the way to you being declared a resident and saving many thousands of dollars by forgoing payment of out-of-state tuition.

Finally, if you're a teen or young adult who is thinking about relocating to another state and being declared as an independent student, check with a school's guidelines first before making any move. Regardless of your level of independence, certain institutions consider you to be a dependent of your parents until you reach a certain age, most often between 19 and 24. Some students may be able to prove otherwise; but recognize that doing so is usually an arduous process.

To learn more about what's required in different parts of the country, check out the college financial aid website called Finaid.org, which has handy links to state residency rules at various institutions.

5. Go to a Flat-tuition School

Private colleges and universities usually charge the same tuition rate to in-state students as well as non-residents.

But one strategy to conquer the problem of out-of-state tuition at public schools is to pass on institutions with tuition surcharges and opt instead for a campus that has just one tuition rate for both residents and non-residents. These public colleges and universities are sometimes known as "flat tuition" schools. But their tuition model can best be described as "one student, one rate."

Examples of flat rate tuition schools that benefit non-residents include the University of Minnesota, Morris, and another Minnesota public college, Bemidji State University. In the 2014-2015 academic year, Bemidji State charged tuition and fees of $8,140 to all students, regardless of their residency.

Likewise, Wilmington University in Delaware does not charge tuition based on where a student resides. Residents and non-residents alike pay equal tuition that is based on which of the school's four campuses students attend.

Note that these schools' tuition structure is different from two other forms of "flat tuition" offered by many schools.

Some institutions guarantee a "flat tuition" to students by locking in fixed pricing for four or five years without any tuition hikes. As explained in Chapter 2, this can benefit residents and non-residents alike. So campuses offering this option may be more attractive if you go out of state.

Another type of "flat tuition" model refers to colleges that don't charge tuition on a "per credit" basis. Instead, these institutions impose one set amount of tuition for full time students, regardless of how many units or credits you take. Most commonly, schools with this pricing structure allow students to take anywhere from 12 to 20 credits. No matter the number of credits or courses taken within those guidelines, students will pay the same flat tuition price. For those willing to take extra classes during the academic year, this type of "flat rate" tuition model can result in thousands of dollars in savings and even allow students to graduate in three years. Like the other "flat tuition" deals, this pricing model also benefits residents as well as out-of-state students.

Unfortunately, if you're looking for a "one student, one rate" type of campus, there aren't a huge number of flat tuition schools from which to choose. Due to economic circumstances, their numbers have dwindled as some colleges have shifted away from this model in recent years.

For instance, Eastern Oregon University was previously a flat rate school that charged all students about $7,000 in tuition. But starting in the 2012-2013 school year, it began charging non-resident tuition. Luckily, students from two states — Idaho and Washington — continue to be charged resident tuition rates. Also, some other students were grandfathered in and locked in resident rates at the campus. For the 2014-2015 school year, those non-residents secured a more than $10,000 discount since resident tuition at Eastern Oregon University was $6,030 and non-resident tuition stood at $16,110.

6. Get Institutional Scholarships to Waive Out-of-state Tuition

If you earn full scholarships to some institutions, many of those schools, like The University of North Carolina system, will give you an added bonus for your accomplishment: they'll let you be classified for tuition purposes as a resident, allowing you to pay resident tuition. In effect, the full scholarship you are granted may cover only in-state tuition rates. But as a scholarship winner, you would not be hit with the tuition surcharge typically imposed on out-of-state students.

As you can see, being an outstanding student who lands a scholarship can help you overcome the problem of high out-of-state tuition.

Even if you don't earn a full scholarship or a complete waiver of out-of-state tuition, some schools, such as Texas A&M University and the University of Arkansas waive portions of out-of-state tuition for scholarship winners.

At many institutions, you don't have to apply for scholarships. You're automatically considered when you submit your admissions application. But if an extra application is required, it's completely worth it to apply for campus or department- specific scholarships, since winning one could help you forgo out-of-state tuition expenses.

7. Take Advantage of Your Public Service Benefits

Have you performed certain community work, such as serving as a Peace Corps volunteer? If so, certain states offer in-state tuition rates to non-residents returning from the Peace Corps.

To discover whether your state of interest offers this tuition break, and other educational benefits, check with the appropriate state's department of education or your local Returned Peace Corps Volunteers chapter.

One great aspect of the Peace Corps' Paul D. Coverdell Fellows Program is that you have lifetime eligibility to get tuition breaks on graduate studies at more than 70 universities. So even if you go back to school later in life, you can take advantage of discounted tuition thanks to your Peace Corps service.

8. Get Tuition Reductions for Special Circumstances

Out-of-state students should always seek tuition discounts and waivers based on special circumstances that may be applicable to them, their parents or other relatives.

For instance, tons of schools offer 100% tuition waivers or reductions in tuition to veterans, military members and their families, as well as students whose parents work in civil service (i.e. firefighters, police or academics).

Tuition breaks in the form of scholarships are also frequently available to students whose family members were alumni, even if the student had been living out of state. Remember the legacy tuition benefits described in Chapter 2? With some alumni scholarships, your *parents* need not have always attended certain colleges and universities. Some institutions — like Seton Hall, Southern Illinois University, and St. John's College — will give you a tuition reduction or an alumni scholarship if your *grandparents* or even a *sibling* went to the school.

The key is to do your homework and also make direct inquiries about any and all tuition reduction programs a school might offer. BestColleges.com publishes a list of 50 colleges with the lowest out-of-state tuition.

Over the past two chapters, we've covered two-dozen ways to cut tuition. If you're diligent in your efforts, and follow the guidance I've provided, you can definitely find a tuition reduction strategy that will work for you.

Now it's time to devote some attention to knocking out the litany of upfront fees that many colleges and universities charge students of all levels.

CHAPTER 4

FIGHTING BACK AGAINST COLLEGE FEES

Tuition and fees can often be lumped together in higher education costs. But just like you should know all the "extras" you're paying for when you buy a car, so too should you be aware of all the additional fees that are charged to you beyond tuition expenses.

For starters, it's important to realize that schools can dream up any kind of "fee." Some schools tie a laundry list of fees to each and every service or benefit they provide to students, regardless of how many students utilize those benefits. Other colleges and universities seem to invent random fees for no other reason than to raise revenues.

You'd certainly notice a $500 fee on your bill, and you'd probably question that charge if you didn't know why it was levied. But would you do the same thing for a $5.00 charge — or even a $0.50 fee?

Regardless of their purpose, at first glance, all these small fees may seem tiny and insignificant. But the problem, all too frequently, is that the ever-growing hodgepodge of so-called "little" fees can snowball over time. They can amass in dollar amounts and in terms of the number of fees being levied. Over the course of your four-year college career, these fees wind up costing you major dollars.

It certainly doesn't help that fees are often presented as a single item, or at best, a group of fees on your student statements and bills. Although some schools do break out fees in detail, most don't. School officials know that parents and students alike would probably become even more enraged about fees if they saw how much nickel and diming was taking place.

So how can you go about keeping a lid on fees?

Your best bet is to attack the issue in five ways:

1. Get fee waivers where possible
2. Just say no to "optional" fees
3. Avoid penalty fees
4. Do some fee sleuthing
5. Become a "fee activist"

At most colleges and universities, health insurance is required as a condition of enrollment. Because of this mandate, schools will frequently automatically enroll students in their campus health insurance plan and charge a fee for that health insurance.

That fee can range from a few hundred bucks to $2,000 or so.

This is one of the largest fees tacked on to many college bills, but it's also one that can be easily waived.

You simply need to have private health insurance and show evidence of such coverage to your college or university. In most cases, parents already have their dependent children covered on their healthcare policy, so this coverage, which typically extends for the student up to age 26, will be sufficient to eliminate or waive the health insurance charge a school imposes.

Says Chrissi Lockwood, the mom whose daughter is now attending the University of Delaware: "On Kati's bill, there was a health insurance fee of $676 for the fall and then $797 for the spring. Had I not waived out of that she would have gotten charged more than $1,400. So parents need to be aware of that."

You can also get waivers from certain fees during specific times, such as when you're away from your home campus, studying abroad or doing field research. Ditto for students who are registered for only off-campus or online classes for an entire semester or longer.

Under these circumstances, schools may waive their "student services" fee or various "campus activity" fees. After all, if you're not even studying on campus — let alone residing in the state for a semester or even a year — you're clearly not taking advantage of those "student services" and "campus activities."

If you obtain a waiver or deferment of fees, you'll typically see the amount credited reflected on your college billing statement.

Also know that many schools, especially state and public schools, have policies in place that specifically provide fee waivers for certain groups of students: like college employees, military members and veterans.

* * *

Healthcare, student services, technology fees and charges for various facilities are perhaps the four most common categories of fees charged by many colleges and universities. But remember, there can be any number of fees that you'll face while earning a college degree.

For instance, at the University of California, Santa Cruz, the school outlines more than 30 different fees — on top of tuition — that are charged each year.

As of this writing, a dozen of those fees were as follows:

- a $2.25 "student voice and empowerment" fee
- a $2.25 "free/anonymous" HIV testing fee
- a $6 theater arts fee
- a $15 intercollegiate athletic sports team fee
- an $18 campus sustainability program fee
- a $24 campus childcare fee
- a $30 student government fee
- a $45 fitness facilities fee
- an $81 student health center expansion fee
- a $90 student facilities fee
- a $120 seismic safety fee
- a $335 transportation fee

All told, the 30-plus fees at UC Santa Cruz added up to more than $4,000. Although UC Santa Cruz may seem like an extreme case, in many ways it's not. Unfortunately, a slew of fees have become the rule in higher education, rather than the exception, especially at public colleges and universities.

At the University of Illinois at Urbana-Champaign, a look at the school's main website pages showing tuition and fees shows that the 2014-2015 base tuition price was $12,036 and fees were $3,566. Just eight categories of fees were listed. But if you drill down farther, you'll also find a breakdown of one category, labeled "student-initiated fees." These expenses, the university says, were actually 10 different fees consolidated starting in the fall 2012 term. "The amount will appear as a single line item on the Student Account and is not refundable," the school's website states.

Just Say No to "Optional" Fees

Remember my earlier analogy about car buying and paying for college? I used that language for a reason — mainly because, as unsavory as it might seem, it's actually an apt comparison.

When you go to buy a new vehicle, many auto dealers try to slap on all kinds of "optional" items, fancy extras and accessories. Such "upgrades" can include anything from glass-etching of a vehicle identification number to souped-up car packages featuring leather interior and fancy trim. Depending on your preferences, these are sometimes "nice to have" items, but they certainly don't fall into the category of "need to have."

The same is true for certain bells and whistles that colleges can creatively push on you. While they may not push them with the same slickness of a car salesman, college officials nonetheless may try to slide their own "optional" fees right past you if you're not careful.

What kind of fees could you find?

Charges for sports packages and yearbooks are common. So too are fees to pay for campus newspapers, research projects and renewable energy programs on college campuses, as well as certain room and facility usage fees (such as fitness centers). Other fees involve entertainment activities (such as tickets to theater productions or discounts for performing arts centers), and charges for student speaker series. Many campuses in the California state system charge optional fees for towels, locks and lockers. Decline all of those and keep a few extra bucks.

When you see any of these kinds of charges, or another type of fee that is not mandatory, know that you can have those items struck from your bill if you simply request it.

Avoid Penalty Fees

Another way that colleges stick you with excessive or unnecessary fees is by imposing penalty charges on some students. More often than not, penalty fees are assessed when someone fails to meet a deadline.

So right off the bat, you can save yourself both frustration and money by simply keeping abreast of any and all college deadlines and then meeting those deadlines.

Better yet, try to be early to further reduce your risk of getting hit with a late fee. You never know when someone might lose your paperwork, or some other unforeseen situation occurs that throws into question whether or not you met some deadline.

Keeping copies of all your college records or getting receipts for your transactions, submissions or online registration activities can also help make sure you won't be penalized unfairly with extra fees in the event of any mishap.

That's important because most fee waivers typically apply only to regular fees that are assessed to students; not to penalty fees such as late registration, or to special program fees, or course-specific fees.

But even if you get hit with a late fee — say because you didn't register for classes on time, or you didn't pay a deposit when required — some schools will retroactively remove those charges if you have a good reason for doing so.

For instance, the University of California, San Diego stipulates that late fees can be removed in two instances, due to:

- University responsibility, which involves action or inaction by the university that causes the delay in enrollment or fee payment; and
- Failure to act by student because of a sudden disabling illness or accident.

So it's certainly not unheard of for late fees to get waived under reasonable circumstances.

Do Some Fee Sleuthing Before Applying

The best time to avoid fees is before you're asked to pay them. Unfortunately, a lot of students and parents are in the dark about college fees, mainly because they haven't done adequate homework to investigate any potential fees.

It's not enough to look on a school's website, for instance, and see what the base tuition rate is or what the collective amount of fees are for a college.

You should have a very good idea of the variety or types of fees a school charges — and most of this information is made public. It's admittedly not very easy to find. But it is there for those willing to do the necessary online digging.

Did you know that at University of Massachusetts Amherst, the flagship campus in the state's public school system, fees are actually higher than tuition?

For about a decade, Massachusetts has largely held tight to tuition, perhaps leading some parents to think that college costs aren't escalating that much. But fees have risen dramatically.

At UMass Amherst, undergraduate fees for 2014-2015 totaled $11,544 for residents, while tuition was just $1,714 for students. Incredibly, this means fees are *seven times higher* than tuition! That doesn't even take into account other "one-time" charges that students at the school incurred. Those fees were another $872.

The same trend holds true at most other state schools in Massachusetts as well.

How do I know this? Because I've tracked down their tuition and fee information and read their policies in detail.

You can do the same thing for any college or university you're considering.

As you search a school's website, look up commonly used phrases like "approved fees" and/or "breakdown of tuition and fees."

By scouring UNC Chapel Hill's website, I found a single critical link, via the finance department, which took me to the following:

All Approved Student Fees
Approved Student Application Fees
Approved Student Debt Service Fees
Approved Student General Fees
Approved Student Miscellaneous Fees
Approved Student Special Fees
Approved Student Activity Fees

Each link takes the reader to a different page that outlines various fees. I've saved you the trouble of counting all the myriad fees (I've already done it).

There are 24 separate fees that all students at Carolina must pay. The fees are just shy of $2,000. In addition, there are a host of other potential fees that could pop up depending on a student's grade level, area of study, and other factors.

Should we all have to become sleuths just to hunt down these higher education costs? Honestly, no, we shouldn't *have* to do so. But the reality is that we *need* to in order to become more informed consumers who are far better prepared for total college costs.

And these aren't the only fees you can expect. All colleges have numerous other "hidden" fees, as I'll explain in detail in Chapter 8.

Become a Fee Activist

Once you become aware of all of these upfront fees, you're better equipped to do something about them. After all, you can't challenge a fee if you don't even know it exists.

One way to fight back against "fee mania" at many colleges is to make your voice heard.

Because most public schools are state supported, they're required to be at least somewhat transparent in their dealings and to provide at least a certain amount of disclosure of fees. Obviously, some schools are far more transparent than others.

Regardless of how open your school might be, you can glean relevant insights just by staying abreast of what happens annually among tuition decision-makers and influencers. Many public institutions, and private schools too, have a "student fee advisory committee" or a "fee taskforce." The members of these committees are campus staff and faculty, state education officials, and often students as well, such as a student body treasurer or student body president.

If you feel passionate about keeping tuition and fees down (and why shouldn't we all feel that way?) you might try going to some committee meetings or even taking a shot at sitting on the committee as a student or public representative.

There is a nationwide need for more strong advocates of affordable higher education.

It's easy to feel like you have to automatically write a check or whip out a credit card when tuition and fees are due.

That's why you don't want to be financially surprised by these charges, no matter whether they're crazy sounding fees or fees with nice-sounding names, like the "student success fees" at the 23-campus California State University system.

Do push back on such charges. Let your school know your concerns. And certainly, if you come across questionable fees, there's no harm in also looking for what loopholes and exemptions may be available to help you avoid those fees.

As it turns out, colleges often treat fee waivers just like they do the multitude of fees they charge: both can be obscured and buried somewhat unless you're willing to hunt for them.

So if there's one thing I hope you'll remember, it's that just because a fee waiver or exemption hasn't been well publicized by a school, that doesn't mean it doesn't exist.

Let's move on now to the next category of upfront fees you must tackle in college: room and board.

CHAPTER 5

ROOM AND BOARD

For many undergraduates in America, one of the biggest thrills of heading off to college is living on their own — and establishing a lot more independence from their parents.

When students go away to college, they often have grand ideas about what college life will be like. Some picture a serious academic environment, complete with all-nighters in the library or dorm. At the other extreme, some kids look forward to being at a "party school," and all that it entails.

No matter what type of college environment they enter, all students have to answer one fundamental question: where will I live when I attend school?

The question has a lot of implications. There are social factors to take into account, family preferences to weigh and — of course — financial considerations.

Room and board expenses at public four-year colleges now average $9,498 nationwide, more than the average tuition costs of $8,893 at public institutions, according to the latest data available from the College Board. That trend — of housing and meal costs exceeding tuition — has actually been in place for several decades.

So understanding a variety of housing issues is critical to managing one's finances and avoiding college debt.

Thankfully, those who can keep a level head about campus housing can fare just fine, even as they deal with escalating room and board fees.

In this chapter, I'll share seven do's and don'ts that will help you to better manage room and board costs. Two of these suggestions can get you completely free housing. The other five recommendations will aid you in keeping student housing from ruining your budget after you've settled in at your chosen school.

So without further adieu, here are seven ways to keep college room and board expenses under control:

1. Do weigh the pros and cons of living at home
2. Do remember the #1 rule of real estate
3. Don't try to upgrade your lifestyle
4. Don't live solo
5. Do forgo all-you-can-eat meal plans
6. Don't forget to strive for housing scholarships
7. Do consider becoming a resident advisor

1. Do Weigh the Pros and Cons of Living at Home

According to data from UCLA, 83% of students live away from home. Only 17% live with parents or relatives. The vast majority of students, 77%, live in campus dorms.

Here is a breakdown of where students live when they go away to college as freshmen:

In a College Dorm — 76.9%
With Parents or Relatives — 17.3%
Other Private Home, Apartment or Room — 2.5%
Other Campus Student Housing — 2.4%
In a Fraternity or Sorority House — 0.6%
Other — 0.3%

Source: UCLA American Freshman survey

Despite the overwhelming number of young adults who leave home to attend college, some students automatically consider living at home because they think it will be cheaper.

In some ways they're right. But in other ways, they're dead wrong.

It's definitely the case that staying at home means the family doesn't have to spend money on additional housing costs for a dorm or an apartment near campus. But it's also the case that students who live at home have far lower graduation rates, and when they do complete school, it takes the much longer to do so.

Research suggests that there are three primary drawbacks faced by those who choose to forgo a residential campus experience.

For starters, living at home diminishes a student's ability to be more actively engaged on campus — limiting time to meet with professors at set office times (or even on an impromptu basis), and limiting time spent hanging out in the library, or just connecting with other like-minded students.

It's also the case that many students who live at home have less "intensity" in their school work, meaning they're more likely to go to school part-time, instead of full-time.

Finally, research shows that many students who live at home while in school often do so simply because they picked a nearby college for convenience rather than quality or fit. But just because a college or university is conveniently located close to your residence, that does not mean that it's a quality institution, nor will convenience alone provide any guarantee that a "nearby" school is the best academic or financial fit.

For all these reasons, living at home typically has the effect of slowing down academic progress for many students.

Those who take longer to graduate (either in part because they live at home or because they need to work more hours) ultimately wind up paying more for higher education. There are additional years of tuition, more fees to pay, as well as the opportunity cost of forgoing work earnings when a student doesn't enter the job market as planned.

Therefore, I'd suggest re-thinking the "stay at home" strategy. There are other ways to cut college costs, as described throughout *College Secrets*. There are also additional ways to shave housing expenses if that's your primary concern.

2. Do Remember the #1 Rule of Real Estate

Although about 40% of students say they and their parents cover tuition expenses, about 60% of students and parents pay for housing.

When asked who is responsible for covering the cost of housing, 30% of students say their parents pay; 31% of students say they pay it themselves; 5% say that a scholarship covers the cost; and 15% say that financial aid funds their housing costs, according to a study by Citigroup and *Seventeen* magazine.

Since housing is a cost that is increasingly being borne by families, it pays to remember one of the number one rules of real estate: location, location, location.

In summary, realize that the location of the school you want to attend will dominate above all other factors when it comes to determining room and board expenses.

So just like real estate is expensive on the East Coast and West Coasts, so too is college housing in these areas. As a result, if you're planning to go to school in a place like New York City, Los Angeles, or the San Francisco bay area, expect your housing costs to be significantly higher than what other students pay at colleges in other parts of the country.

Beatrice Schultz is a Certified Financial Planner and the founder of Westface College Planning. She is also the host of College Smart Radio — Tackling the Runaway Costs of College — a weekly radio show on 1220am KDOW, The Wall Street Business Network.

She says she sees families making costly mistakes when it comes to college housing all the time.

"People make a huge error in assuming that the main cost of attendance is tuition. In some cases room and board is more than the actual tuition," Schultz said, citing UC Berkeley, which she said has some of the most expensive student housing in the country. For 2014-2015, room and board rates at Cal Berkeley ran from a low of $14,000 to a high of $18,210. But in-state tuition at Berkeley was only about $6,000.

Other college experts echo Schultz's sentiment.

"The main reason why people who go to public universities end up in debt, is not the tuition, but the living away from home expenses, which at a public university, are three or four times more than tuition," said

Andrew Hacker, co-author of *Higher Education? How Colleges are Wasting Our Money And Failing Our Kids — And What We Can Do About It*, in a Fiscal Times report on hidden college costs.

According to The College Board's Trends In College Pricing survey, room and board fees for the 2013-2014 academic term throughout the United States were as follows:

Southwest:	$7,831
South:	$8,562
Midwest:	$ 8,737
New England:	$10,544
Middle States:	$11,041
West:	$11,346

The data show that a student attending college in the West — like California, Hawaii or Washington — will pay $3,515 extra, or 45% more in room and board, than the typical student attending a school in the Southwest. That's an added cost of $14,060 over four years. Imagine that! By just opting out of a West Coast school in favor of an institution in the Southwest, you could save a small fortune.

Furthermore, a student going to school in Middle states — such as New York, New Jersey or Pennsylvania — will pay $2,479, or 29% more in room and board fees than a student attending a school in the South. That's nearly $10,000 more spent while earning a bachelor's degree.

And a student attending a college or university in the New England area — including Connecticut, Massachusetts and New Hampshire — will shell out $1,807, or 21% more, than students pursuing degrees in the Midwest. That's a difference of more than $7,200 during a four-year education.

So to knock back pricey dorm fees, college-bound students shouldn't omit affordable real estate markets, including the Southwest, South, Midwest, and rural areas and zones outside of major metropolitan districts.

To illustrate this point, consider Eastern New Mexico University, a school whose total published cost for the 2014-2015 school year was only $12,750 for residents and just over $18,500 for non-residents. That includes tuition, fees, room and board. The university's costs are so low largely thanks to very affordable room and board charges totaling less than $6,500 a year. Wise up, students: save money by making smarter "real estate" decisions.

3. Don't Try to Upgrade Your Lifestyle

What is your image of what a college lifestyle is supposed to be, especially college housing?

In decades past, students hunkered down in bunk beds, most often with two to four people in a tiny room, and gladly ate ramen or beans and rice as they studied (or even partied) their way through college.

But these days, many residential units for students seem to mirror — or even top — what most American kids experience at home.

The New York Times has written about some of the ways that student housing luxuries now overshadow studying in certain off-campus housing complexes in many college towns.

The Times highlighted the fact that amid so much competition, housing developers are looking for ways to set their student housing units apart.

"That has led to the construction of complexes with tanning salons; spas offering manicures, pedicures, facials and massages; 24-hour workout rooms with virtual trainers; and outdoor pools with bars and cabanas. There are washers and dryers that send text messages when a cycle is complete, and exercise machines that allow users to check their e-mail," the Times noted.

Where are all these fancy off-campus housing units?

One of them opened in 2013 in Austin, Texas. A private developer called American Campus Communities, which owns or manages nearly 200 properties, constructed the new 17-story complex, called Callaway House.

To make the facility a standout, the developer teamed up with a network service provider to outfit this student housing complex with Internet speeds of up to one-gigabit per resident.

One gigabit is about 100 times faster than the average home cable-modem connection. That lightning-fast one gigabit Internet service is believed to be the first of its kind in a residence hall in the United States.

As the Chronicle of Higher Education noted, Callaway House also boasts an array of other amenities, including "a rooftop fitness center, a swimming pool, and a full-service dining facility. The building has 661 beds in regular suites and 92 beds in 'penthouse' units on the top two floors, where students are promised 'upgraded interior finishes, 'wow-inspiring views,' and 'the privacy and lifestyle you deserve.'"

Despite all these cushy amenities, some educators say there's something decidedly lacking in many upscale off-campus student properties: the kind of housing environment typically found on a college or university campus, including work spaces and study rooms — not to mention libraries, halls and auditorium-style gathering places that can host lectures or promote lively academic discussions.

In other words, there's often not a whole lot of intellectual stimulation going on in a luxury off-campus housing complex. And with colleges and universities increasingly cracking down on under-age drinking, some parents believe that certain students just want to live off campus in order to have the freedom to consume alcohol.

* * *

On campus, the race is also on at many colleges and universities that want to build posh dorms. These college-based dorms may not have some of the over-the-top amenities as off-campus housing providers boast — like rooftop pools, on-site restaurants or bars, and apartments decked out with flat-screen TVs and granite countertops, but schools are upgrading dramatically to try to capture what they think students and parents want and demand.

From the standpoint of many schools, they feel it's in their best interest to stay one step ahead in the luxury dorm race. Without top-notch residential facilities, or at least very livable modern housing units, schools think students will be turned off.

I can't say that I disagree with that notion, based on personal experience, conversations with students, and research into this topic. However, I believe it's a mistake for students to try to upgrade their lifestyles when they venture off to college. In my view, fancy luxuries and upscale amenities should come much later — as in after a student graduates and gets a job.

Nevertheless, on the numerous campus tours we took, my teen daughter was quick to point out any subpar dorms. She also lit up like a firecracker at seeing high-end dorms, like the plush facilities at Fordham University's Lincoln Center campus.

Fordham opened the doors to brand new, penthouse level apartments/dorms in the fall of 2014. The dorms are housed in a modern, eco-friendly residential tower that accommodates 400 undergraduate students. The new building touts modern bedroom suites, common living spaces, study lounges, a movie theatre, a dining hall, and, naturally, to-die-for views of New York City. Those fabulous digs, as you might suspect, also come at a hefty price.

Double or triple room rates at the New Residence Hall at Lincoln Center, which only houses first-year students, were set at $11,545 for the 2014-2015 academic year. Freshman meal plans ranged from $5,350 to $6,250 per school year, bringing total room and board expenses to as much as $17,795.

Housing at Fordham's older Lincoln Center residential facility — which is called McMahon Hall and is only for sophomores, juniors, seniors, law and graduate students — features fully furnished two- and three-bedroom apartments with living rooms. Room rates alone there for 2014-2015 were $14,630 for a double room and $17,095 for a single room, making Fordham one of the priciest residential campuses in America.

Fordham and other colleges around the country are no doubt aware of research into dorms and student preferences. One study published by the Association of Higher Education Facilities Officers put it bluntly. It stated that "poorly maintained or inadequate residential facilities" was the number-one reason students rejected enrolling at institutions.

With that kind of information in the back — no, make that the *fore-front* — of campus administrators' minds, I expect upgraded dorms to become more of a trend in the years ahead. That's almost certain to be the case at America's top tier colleges and universities, where housing fees continue to climb.

For these reasons, families should re-think demanding that colleges have "better lifestyle" features, such as "fancier meals, food courts and recreational amenities like climbing walls," says economist and college expert Lucie Lapovsky.

4. Don't Live Solo

It's amazing how some teens can survive the first 18 years of life sharing a bedroom with a sister or brother, or sometimes even two siblings. But then when they're planning to attend college, these teens want nothing more than to live *completely* on their own.

Big mistake. Colleges charge fat premiums for students who live by themselves. Some schools won't even allow freshmen to bunker down solo.

That's a good policy because it's in the student's best interests — academically, socially and financially — to have a roommate.

Part of college life is learning how to get along with others, and yes, that includes strangers that you've never previously met. That is a skill that will also be required in the workforce where you'll have to work in teams and do projects with others who haven't been your best friends since 5th grade. Moreover, roommates can be helpful sounding boards, study mates, social buddies, or just people to walk with to the dining hall with as students get adjusted to campus life.

Needless to say, having a roommate also significantly cuts your rooming charges. Double occupancy units will be far less than singles. Triples, with three students, will be even cheaper than doubles. And if you can stand it, quads are the most economical housing arrangement of all within most campus dorms and apartments.

Some schools even let a 5th student reside in a dorm or apartment. That's the case at Stockton College in New Jersey, where students living in campus apartments with five students instead of four get an additional 15% discount.

"I'm always flabbergasted by the people who say they can't afford college but can somehow come up with money for the single room or the highest price dorm on campus," Lapovsky says.

Remember that when you're trying to cut college costs.

5. Do Forgo All-you-can-eat Meal Plans

Besides the cost of living in a dorm or campus apartment, you'll also have to pay for food. No one can study effectively on an empty stomach, right?

Well, you definitely want to be well fed and nourished when you're a college student. But you don't have to go to two opposite extremes either: gorging yourself just because food is available or wasting money paying for food you'll never eat.

Either problem can occur for students who have "all you can eat" meal plans. You've heard of that expression: "the freshman 15," right? It refers to the 15 pounds that students often gain during their first year of college. Some weight gain could just be from hitting the books so much that students stop being as active as they were in high school, when mandatory physical education classes were the norm. But some students may see weight creep because they're eating a lot of junk food, or they're simply eating too much. All-you-can-eat or "unlimited" meal plans may encourage constant snacking and over-indulgence. Why stop at three meals a day and snacks, when you can go on some campuses for a 24-hour pizza run, and it's "free" as part of your meal plan? Do you get my point?

Health issues aside, many students find that once they get into the rhythm of college life, they simply don't eat three meals and multiple snacks each day. Some are just fine to eat a late breakfast and an early dinner. Others meter out meals based on their sleeping schedule and class load. Whatever the case, know that many schools offer mid-range eating plans — such as 14 to 20 meals per week. For a lot of students, this is just fine in an average 7-day period. For those who actually find themselves hungry later, they can always bump up their meal plans. But it's best to start off conservatively, save money, and see what the student's eating habits truly entail.

6. Don't Forget to Strive for Housing Scholarships

A final way to slash your housing expenses is to strive for housing scholarships. The way you do this, quite simply, is by being the very best student you can possibly be.

Earning a housing scholarship usually requires excellence, and many colleges and universities award free housing on a very competitive basis.

Take Morehead State University, in Morehead, KY, for instance. The university grants about 100 full tuition and university housing scholarships each year via its Presidential Scholarship Program.

The awards go primarily to National Merit Scholars, Semi-Finalists and Finalists, valedictorians, as well as high-performing students with top grades and stellar standardized test scores.

Any school you're considering that offers merit aid may also provide housing scholarships. They award these sought-after funds to the very best students who apply.

To find such a housing scholarship, do some online research for the college or university you're interested in or are already attending.

Many schools use similar names to describe their top academic awards, including those with full tuition and housing allowances. Among these awards are: "Presidential Scholarships" "University Scholarships" "Chancellor's Scholarships" "Regents Scholarships" "Dean's Scholarships" and "Founders Scholarships."

If you nab a "full ride" scholarship — one that covers tuition, fees, room and board — all your worries about those upfront college expenses will likely melt away.

7. Do Consider Becoming a Resident Advisor

Resident advisers are students who live and work in dormitories and other campus-based housing complexes. An "R.A.," as they're called, works by helping other students deal with a number of issues. An R.A. could be called upon to help settle a roommate dispute, to open a locked door for a student who forgot his room key, or to arrange events in the common spaces of the dorm.

Most R.A.s are juniors and seniors in college, though some are sophomores or even graduate students. Freshmen don't serve as R.A.s for obvious reasons — they're newbies who are just getting to know a campus.

But after you've been around a school for a year or longer, it's worth considering becoming an R.A. Not only will you get to know most students in your housing unit — or at least on your floor — you'll also get to save money on housing expenses. That's because an R.A. typically receives either free room and board, or a housing allowance to partially cover room charges.

At least one of these seven strategies is bound to work for you when it comes to cutting room and board expenses at your college or university. In fact, if you use multiple strategies in combination, you'll save even more cash year after year.

Now let's look at the final category of upfront expenses you'll have to contend with in college: books and supplies.

CHAPTER 6

$\mathcal{B}$OOKS AND $\mathcal{S}$UPPLIES

The latest data from the College Board show that college students spend about $1,200 a year on books and supplies.

That's a lot of cash. But believe it or not, the National Association of College Stores reports that spending on college textbooks is actually on the decline.

Textbook expenditures are heading south due to two factors: technology, as well as the overall demand (by students and some colleges alike) for greater affordability.

On the technology front, some colleges are actually providing textbooks free of charge and exploring alternatives to those enormous and enormously expensive textbooks of a generation ago.

Nevertheless, 40% of U.S. families still report being surprised by certain college expenses — and the most common culprits are college textbooks, supplies and equipment, according to a Sallie Mae survey.

To avoid certain unwanted financial surprises, here are 13 strategies that will save you lots of money on college textbooks and supplies.

1. Consider not buying certain textbooks
2. Check books out from the library — any library
3. Use open source textbooks
4. Swap or barter
5. Share books with another student
6. Avoid the campus bookstore
7. Get the international version
8. Use an older edition
9. Buy used books

10. Try e-books
11. Rent textbooks
12. Go directly to the publisher
13. Sell your books after the course

Let's start with the first five strategies, all of which can help you get textbooks completely free of charge.

1. Consider Not Buying Textbooks at All

One of the biggest mistakes students make — and then later regret — is loading up on tons of brand-spanking new textbooks and then later discovering that there are certain texts that they never really used. Sometimes students' books will literally still have the plastic wrap around them at the end of the semester, because they weren't essential to the class, and were never cracked open.

How is this possible? Are these students just goofing off and not studying? Actually no. It's simply that textbooks may not be absolutely mandatory for learning, testing or other forms of academic engagement.

Class notes from faculty lectures may be far more important, group projects or fieldwork may be emphasized, or films and other in-class assignments may take center stage. But it's hard to know this until you've actually sat through a course — unless, that is, you do some preliminary homework on what the class entails.

So the very first step in controlling textbook expenses is to figure out whether you really and truly need a given book at all.

The syllabus for a class usually gives you the first hint.

If a book is designated as "recommended reading," it's not mandatory and likely won't get much use. It could just be a text that the professor thinks may be of interest or is merely supplementary to the heart of classroom activity.

On the other hand, books labeled as "required reading" are typically far more important. But even then, not every text declared as "required" turns out to be essential.

Either way, once you know what class you're taking, it's a smart idea to e-mail the professor and ask directly whether a given book on a syllabus is actually necessary for the class. For additional perspective, you can also ask a student who has just taken the course how necessary he or she found the book. Such feedback can be valuable. But do heed, first and foremost, what the professor has to say.

Some professors will tell you flat-out that certain books on a syllabus really *aren't* essential. Others will say various texts *are* absolutely necessary. Either way, at least you know upfront what to expect. Armed with this knowledge, you can possibly save money by forgoing a book purchase altogether if it's clear that a book won't be critical, or even mildly helpful, to your studies.

If it's not indicated in your syllabus, also ask your professor for three other key pieces of information: the ISBN for the book, any online lab codes you might need for additional materials, and info on any CDs or DVDs that are required with the text.

2. Check Books Out from The Library — Any Library

If you truly need to get your hands on a copy of an essential textbook for a class, libraries may turn out to be your single best sources of free materials.

Savvy students save many hundreds of dollars per semester by borrowing mandatory textbooks, and most students get the books from their own campus library.

You can usually do this in several ways. First, the book might be available for normal checkout, and you can keep it for a few weeks and renew it as often as necessary — provided no one else is demanding the book. Even if you wind up paying a late fee for going past the book's return date, that fine will be a tiny fraction of the book's cost. (In fairness to other students, though, don't hog a book all semester long if there's a waiting list for it).

Alternatively, you can check the Reserve Collection at your college or university's library. The Reserve Collection is a special area (usually near the Circulation desk) where professors leave designated materials for their students. Professors do this because they understand that books are costly and that not everyone can afford to purchase $200 textbooks.

Books held in the Reserve Collection usually have short borrowing periods of just an hour or two. The reason for the tight window is to give as many students as possible the chance to read a popular required textbook.

Books taken from the Reserve area are usually supposed to be read only within the library; meaning you can't take them out of the building. With some classes, there may be exceptions to this general rule, particularly if a professor approves a long-term borrowing option — with "long term" meaning anywhere from a day to perhaps as long as a week.

Professors have been known to also earmark other materials — like DVDs, PowerPoint presentations and audio files — in the Reserve Collection area. Getting these materials on a short-term basis from the library is a great way to save money on books and other necessary supplies.

The Interlibrary Loan System

If you need a specific textbook, but it isn't available in your school's library, you have three options.

You can ask the professor to please request a copy (or an additional copy) for the campus library. Most professors would be more than happy to oblige this request, especially if there was no book put on reserve for the class.

Alternatively, you can take advantage of an under-utilized benefit at many colleges and research universities. That benefit is the interlibrary loan system.

Under this system, your library will tap into the resources of affiliated libraries and see if the book you want is available elsewhere. If a book is located in another library, your campus librarian will arrange to have the book delivered to your school — all at no cost to you.

You can get a host of items through interlibrary loan, including: articles, audio-visual materials, books, book chapters (typically emailed in PDF format, with a one-chapter limit to avoid copyright infringement), dissertations and theses, journals, microfilm, recordings and other materials. You often get to keep these items for several weeks and can renew them as well.

If no other library in your college's interlibrary loan system has the textbook you need, there's nothing to stop you from going to a public library in the city or town in which you live and inquiring about whether they have the book on their shelves.

Certain very large companies have corporate libraries. So if a close relative works for a Fortune 100 firm, he or she likely has borrowing rights and may be able to help you out in a pinch.

Most often, though, you'll just need to go to a nearby public library. If you don't have a library card for your local library, get one pronto! With that public library card, you can take advantage of all their resources — including *their* interlibrary system, which may include connections with other public, academic or corporate libraries not tied to your own campus network.

In the end, it may take some effort to hunt down all your required books, and it's very possible that specific books may not be available through libraries. But when you do find out that a given book does exist within the library system, it's wise to take advantage of this free resource.

As a final note about library books and other borrowed materials, you should obviously treat these items with the utmost care. Don't write notes in books, doodle any funny drawings or highlight any of the text. Keep all library materials in tip-top condition, do your best to observe deadlines, and return library items exactly as you received them.

3. Use Open-source Textbooks

Picture for a moment a world in which students attending college would get all their textbooks completely free. Does it seem like a pipe dream?

Well, it's a lot closer to reality than you might suspect — and not just for students formally enrolled in higher education institutions.

There's a fast-growing movement in the U.S. to dramatically bring down the cost of college textbooks, and even make them totally free to students and others.

If this effort succeeds (and we should all cross our fingers that it does!), students and their families will save small fortunes — now and in the years ahead.

At the heart of this movement are open-source textbooks, also known as "open access textbooks." These are course materials that authors offer free of charge via a nonrestrictive license.

When colleges and universities use open-source books, students benefit from these free educational texts written by college faculty, peer-reviewed and some say, more advantageous than old-fashioned texts. One advantage:

open access books can be easily and quickly updated, without having to wait for a couple years as is often the case with traditional textbooks that need to undergo revisions or corrections.

But the biggest and most obvious benefit of open textbooks is that they're free. And this has a major impact on a student's class choices and overall academic success.

A study released by the U.S. PIRG Education Fund found that American students would do far better academically if they all had free and open textbooks. The study was called "Fixing the Broken Textbook Market: How Students Respond to High Textbook Costs and Demand Alternatives."

Among the study's findings:

- 65% of students choose not to buy a college textbook because it's too expensive.
- 94% report that they suffer academically because they don't have a book.
- 48% say they changed which classes they took based on textbook costs, either taking fewer classes or enrolling in different classes.
- 82% of students say they would do significantly better in a course if the textbook were free online and a hard copy was optional.
- Case studies at both Houston Community College and Virginia State University suggest that students in classes using open textbooks have higher grades and better course completion rates.

In light of these facts, even members of Congress are looking into the issue.

Luckily, open textbooks are gaining in popularity among those in the know in academia.

Some schools, like the University of Georgia, are getting behind the effort in a big way. The Center for Teaching and Learning at the University of Georgia has a large Open Educational Resource (OER) initiative that continues to evolve. Under one element of the program, the school decided to stop using a traditional biology book that had been required for two popular biology classes. Instead of assigning the Bio book, which cost nearly $100, educators replaced it with a free, open textbook. That single change saved about $200,000 total for roughly 2,000 students.

Non-profits such as OpenStax College and College Open Textbooks are at the forefront of efforts to promote awareness and use of open textbooks.

OpenStax College is a digital publisher that permits students to download and print free open source books that the organization has created. The books are produced in full color and are peer-reviewed, just like more standard textbooks that cost $100 or more.

OpenStax College's catalog presently includes seven free titles for introductory courses, including anatomy, biology, economics, physics, physiology, sociology, and statistics.

According to the organization, OpenStax College launched in 2012 and the group's first seven books have already saved students more than $9 million, have been downloaded more than 500,000 times, and have been adopted by more than 600 high schools, community colleges, four-year colleges and research universities.

OpenStax College is now in the midst of rolling out what it calls its "biggest-impact titles to date." By the end of 2014, OpenStax College says it will publish additional titles for courses that typically enroll more than a million U.S. students each year.

Among the books slated to debut in late 2014 were new titles for chemistry, pre-calculus, psychology and U.S. history. Eventually, OpenStax College, which is based at Rice University, plans to offer free books covering 25 of the country's most-attended college courses.

Since OpenStax College has backers like the William and Flora Hewlett Foundation, the Bill and Melinda Gates Foundation, the 20 Million Minds Foundation, and other big-name supporters, I fully expect this ambitious non-profit to meet its lofty and admirable goals.

Meantime, for-profit companies like Lumen Learning and Boundless are also assisting colleges and universities in adopting open education resources. Boundless has a platform, for instance, that offers customizable intro-level textbooks in more than 20 subjects.

All this activity has some teachers and professors getting in on the act too, creating their own free textbooks, articles and web-based videos for use by students. Some do this on their own; others use the platforms offered by a variety of players in the open educational resource marketplace.

Proponents of open education share one common goal: they all want knowledge and learning — whether from a book, a lecture, an audiotape or anything else — to be free and open.

According to the group Textbook Equity -- which offers free PDFs of open education, college-level textbooks — the definition of OER is "teaching, learning, and research resources that reside in the public domain or have been released under an intellectual property license that permits their free use or re-purposing by others."

I like to think of it this way, when contemplating what it means to have free, open books:

The "free" part is pretty straightforward. It means no one has to pay anything at all to tap into these educational resources. That fits into the original point of education: for the learned members of a community to freely share their knowledge with others. The "open" part refers to the use of legal tools (i.e. open licenses), giving anyone, anywhere in the world permission to use, reuse or even modify educational resources. (The latter part of the OER movement is a bit more complicated and will no doubt evolve over time.)

For now, just by asking, you can certainly find out if any of your college professors offer their own open source textbooks. Also, check out the Community College Consortium for Open Educational Resources for a list of free online textbooks in various academic areas.

4. Swap or Barter

Swapping and bartering to get the items you need works in virtually every area of life, and it can be effective for getting free college books and supplies, too.

Arranging a swap or barter with a pal at school can be pretty easy. Simply put the word out that there's a specific book or certain supplies you want, and offer something in exchange — like books, tools or supplies that you own and can easily lend out. The swap can be arranged for a fixed period of time, or you can swap items permanently.

To find someone who has what you need, you may have to cast a wide net. To do this, post a notice on campus bulletin boards or on websites like Craigslist; tap into your social network on Facebook, Twitter and elsewhere; let friends or classmates know you want to swap; and inquire with students who are one grade above you, since they may have already taken the class and have the book handy.

If you prefer not to arrange a swap on your own, there's an online marketplace where students swap books. It's called PaperBackSwap.com and it can help you obtain books, as well as get rid of those books you no longer want or need. The service is completely free. You need only pay for low-cost shipping via Media Mail when someone requests one of your books.

Also, note that despite its name, the PaperBackSwap site lets you trade hardback books, textbooks, and audio books, too.

5. Share Books

Here's a final way to get certain books completely free: just share with a classmate or someone taking the course during the same semester. Find out who has a book that you need, and if it's a friend, politely ask whether you can use the book at certain agreed-upon times.

If you do opt to share a book, be clear about the guidelines and who will have the book when. For example, maybe your roommate is taking the same intro History course that you are taking, but you're in the Monday, Wednesday, Friday session and he's in the Tuesday, Thursday class. You could both split the days that you use the book and create a schedule with specific hours on the weekends when you each have the text.

As with anything else, when you're using someone else's property, take good care of it — better care than you might take your own things. Showing respect for another person's items is just good manners and the right thing to do. It can also pay off in spades if you want to borrow something or share again in the future. That individual will know that you can be trusted to properly handle books or other supplies without damaging or losing them.

6. Avoid the Campus Bookstore

Let's assume now that you've exhausted all your free options, but you still need a certain book, or maybe even a couple of books. Where should you begin?

Actually, a better question is: where *shouldn't* you go?

The single worst place to buy college textbooks is the place that's oh-so-easy and convenient: your college bookstore.

There are two main reasons that it's a rotten idea to buy your books from the on-campus bookstore — and both of them have to do with finances.

For starters, college bookstores are notoriously expensive. That book for your Engineering class will probably cost around $200 from your campus bookstore. But you can easily get it for at least 30% off elsewhere.

The same thing is true for books in every academic discipline. College bookstores have huge markups because they know they have a captive audience. You're already right there on campus, so college and university bookstore managers know that — if push comes to shove — you're probably likely to just run in the store and grab what you need for ease of access and convenience's sake alone.

But don't fall for it. With proper planning, you can avoid those killer bookstore prices and get college textbooks more affordably elsewhere.

A second reason to skip the college bookstore is that it can seem like a candy store. Everything looks so sweet, tempting and inviting — including a bunch of stuff that you don't really need and may never use.

Even if it's super cute and oozing with campus spirit, do you really need to buy a shower curtain with your school's mascot emblazoned on it? Or a matching set of table lamps that feature your college or university's name and school colors? Certainly not. And certainly not for two or three times the price that you could get these items elsewhere.

But just being in the college bookstore can feel a bit like window shopping. So sooner or later, if you keep hitting that campus store, you'll probably do the same thing you do as when you go to hang out at the mall intending only to "window shop." You'll end up spending money.

Little wonder then that the National Association of College Stores (NACS) reports that the average full-time student spends about $710 annually in a campus bookstore. Of that total, roughly $420 was spent on books and course materials in the store or on its online site. The rest of the money spent in college stores — nearly $300 — was doled out for everything from insignia apparel and computer products to gifts, supplies and food.

Do yourself a favor by actively avoiding the college bookstore. That will help keep extra cash in your pocket all school year long.

7. Buy the International Version of the Book

Purchasing the international version of a book you need is another big-time money-saver when it comes to college books.

In terms of content, international editions of college textbooks are usually the exact same versions of U.S. editions, sometimes down to the exact page number. When differences do exist, they are very minor.

From a packaging standpoint, there are two differences between U.S. versions of textbooks and their international counterparts. With the latter books, they come in paperback form, rather than hardback, and international versions will almost always be printed in black-and-white throughout, not in color in some sections as may be the case with illustrations, photos and diagrams, or other sections of U.S. versions of a book.

For these differences, wouldn't you say it's worth it to spend $30 on an international book that goes for $130 in the U.S. version? I think so.

Where can you find international versions of college books?

ValoreBooks.com is a great site that sells international editions at a big discount. One reason that customers can get books so cheap this way is that ValoreBooks.com connects buyers with more than 20,000 independent booksellers nationwide selling in excess of 18 million items. All that competition keeps prices low.

BookDepository.com, the U.K.'s largest online bookseller, is another well-regarded site with cheap international versions of college textbooks, as well as other affordable texts. The company ships books for free anywhere in the world — regardless of how much or how little you spend. One factor to take into account, though, is that the company is located in the United Kingdom, so its shipping originates from a Gloucester, U.K. warehouse. That means books usually take a little longer to arrive in the U.S. But not much longer, users say, than getting books from domestic online booksellers. BookDepository.com fulfills all orders within 48 hours.

8. Use an Older Edition

Buying a previous version of a required textbook will typically save you 50% or more off the price you'd spend on a brand new textbook. For many students, older versions of textbooks are just fine when it comes to serving needs in a variety of college courses.

You would think that publishers and authors would put out revised versions or updates of their books only when there are substantial changes needed or there's a significant amount of new information to add to a topic.

Unfortunately, that's hardly the case. Students and professors alike complain that publishers and authors slap a label like "revised version" or "6th edition" on a book even when the overwhelming majority of the information is exactly the same as printed in the previous edition.

So ask a professor whether the revised, newer version of a book is required. Chances are, if a professor has been teaching from a specific text for some time, he or she will know if older versions are perfectly suitable for the class.

If it's a class on ancient Greek Mythology, for instance, is a book from 2008 really going to be much different than the same book republished in 2015?

Ditto for certain areas of math, like calculus, where the content is pretty much the same. Just realize that problem sets or other aspects of older texts could be slightly different than what your peers in class have if they own new textbooks.

One other point of note: Congress passed The Higher Education Act back in 2008, and the law went into effect in 2010. It requires colleges to list the textbooks for various classes at the same time schools open registration. So, in theory, your course catalogues and directories of college classes are supposed to list the texts required for each course whenever possible. When this system is done right, you have the advantage of being able to look up books *before* you even register for the course.

Obviously not all colleges and universities do this.

9. Buy Used Textbooks

Even if a professor insists on a specific version of a book, no one says it has to be a brand-new copy of that text. You can — and should — buy used books whenever possible to save money.

The average used textbook costs 75% of the price of a new book, NACS data show. Other studies show even bigger discounts for used books. Used book sales also make up nearly one-third of all textbooks sales in college stores and that number is on the rise as students get wise to the benefits of used books.

You can get used books from Amazon.com, Craigslist, eBay and eCampus, as well as the other online book retailers previously mentioned in this chapter.

To help scour the landscape for the best deals across multiple textbook sites, check out comparison sites like BIGWORDS, Bookfinder and CampusBooks. They each have tools that let you find new and used book prices by searching a book's title, author, or ISBN. The ISBN will ensure that you receive the right version of a book if you're trying to locate a must-have edition for a class.

10. Consider e-Textbooks

Many college students have e-readers and tablets before they get to college, thanks to the flourishing e-book market. So you'll be happy to know that the e-textbook market is also booming.

Buying e-books can significantly reduce the money you'll spend on textbooks, since they can be as much as 50% to 60% off the price of hardback books. Discounts abound for e-books used in place of paperbacks as well.

Besides their lower price, e-books have other advantages. You can take notes in an e-textbook via your e-reader or other device. You can comfortably carry a lot more books around rather than lugging around a heavy backpack. E-books are also environmentally friendly, since publishers need not print any pages for this textbook format.

If you need to print something from an e-book you're using for a college course, just make sure you know the terms and conditions for printing, as well as any other restrictions or usage rules, such as time limits that might apply.

Most of the sites mentioned throughout this chapter sell e-books. In the low-cost digital category, there are also websites like Flat World Knowledge, which may have a textbook you need that can be viewed online or downloaded at an affordable price.

11. Rent Textbooks

Renting textbooks is yet another option to make sure college books won't put you in the poorhouse.

Rented books cut your textbook costs between 33% and 55% when compared with the price of a new printed text, NACS says.

(Even though most college bookstores offer textbook rentals, you do remember what I said about avoiding campus stores, correct?)

You're better off just renting course materials by ordering them online. Lots of companies do this, and they promise savings of 70% to 90%. Here are some of the places you can rent college textbooks, and keep them for up to a semester:

Alibris
Amazon
Barnes & Noble
BookByte
BookRenter
Campus Book Rentals
Chegg
Textbook Rentals
Textbooks
TextbookStop
ValoreBooks

If the prices are all the same, go with the retailer offering free shipping, preferably both ways. Coupons, special discounts or other perks, like a grace period for late rentals, are other bonuses to seek.

If you want to do a good deed, you might consider using Chegg. In addition to offering rentals at a great price, they plant a tree for every order.

And if you don't want to check rental prices on each site individually, no problem.

You can make sure you're getting a good deal by using a really good aggregator site, PriceRetriever.net, which compares dozens of book retailers, showing you which company has the lowest price.

PriceRetriever is an add-on to your browser that activates on your college's bookstore website. Just install the app or log onto PriceRetriever's site to get started. Using PriceRetriever, you can instantly compare textbook prices at more than 60 retailers, including the cost of new and used books, rentals and e-books.

When placing your textbook rental order, plan ahead and give yourself at least five to seven business days to make sure your books reach you in time.

If you're in a big hurry, try renting an e-book via a site like CourseSmart, which will let you read a textbook online or via a copy-protected PDF. You can also access their content through mobile apps for iOS and Android. Kindle owners or app users can likewise rent textbooks from Amazon in the same fashion.

12. Try Going Through the Publisher's Site Directly

Roughly a century ago, back in 1915, the most expensive textbook around was a Geometry book that cost $2.50. That's about $54 today. But today's average Geometry book sells for roughly $70, according to the group Textbook Equity, which promotes free, open books.

Among all college textbooks, average prices range from $100 to $200, the group says. In the past decade alone, textbook prices shot up 82%, more than three times the rate of inflation.

Why have prices risen so dramatically and disproportionately over the years?

Textbook Equity puts the blame largely on the publishing industry.

"The primary reason that (books) cost so much is the ever increasing concentration of the textbook publishing industry through hundreds of acquisitions, resulting in the elimination of price competition, the established policies of schools that inhibit alternatives sources of textbooks, and somewhat the lack of awareness of professors about the cost of college textbooks they adopt for their classes," Textbook Equity said in a recent blog post.

Since a handful of large publishers dominate the college textbook market, it's easy to see Textbook Equity's point of view.

The U.S. PIRG largely agrees. PIRG officials point out that alternative methods to lower college textbook costs — such as renting books or buying used texts and e-books — can only go so far because the prices of new printed books (which are put out by publishers) underpin the entire textbook marketplace and drive market conditions for all those other lower-cost book options.

Until the situation changes, what can you do when it comes to dealing with this reality? You should first try to use the strategies previously mentioned in this chapter. If none of those work, unfortunately your final option might be a "if you can't beat 'em, join 'em" approach.

What I mean by this is that even though many consumer groups and students alike bash publishers and blame them for the sky-high price of many college textbooks, publishing companies can *occasionally* have lower priced books than you'd find elsewhere. You may be able to get a better price than you would at a college bookstore if you go directly to a book publisher's website.

Some publishers offer web discounts, coupons and other price reductions for all kinds of books, whether you're buying new or used, renting, or searching for an e-book. So it's worth a shot just to check it out and see if a publisher has a special deal going on at the time you need a particular textbook. Obviously, this is a last-ditch strategy and certainly not ideal. But it may save you a few bucks in rare instances.

13. Sell Back Your Books and Supplies

No chapter on books and supplies would be complete if I didn't share one last piece of advice on cutting costs in this area: and that recommendation is to sell your books and supplies to someone else when you no longer need them.

Going to your campus bookstore to do this will get you (almost) nowhere. That $150 book you bought? You're lucky if they'll offer you $20 for it.

So stick to the plan and go elsewhere. Since you're unloading merchandise, you want to try a website that makes it easy to do that, and do it fast.

Sites like Valore Books, with good book buyback programs, are best for this process.

Other good options are eBay or Craigslist, where some sellers fetch higher prices, even if it might take a little longer to get the cash.

But nearly all of the online retailers mentioned in this chapter offer direct book buybacks or a platform for you to sell your books to interested third parties. Scout around a bit and you'll find the best offers in the marketplace.

If you do sell to a third party, be prepared for whatever company you choose to take a cut out of your sales price. Most retailers keep about 10% to 15% of what you make on the sale.

Also, remember that you might change your mind about a book, or later find it cheaper elsewhere. In such instances, you may be able to get a full refund. To help the refund process go smoothly, handle any brand-new books and supplies you've bought with extra special care. Refrain from un-wrapping or writing in your books until you're absolutely certain that you'll keep them. Even if you don't use the materials, once you unwrap books or unbundle merchandise (like a multi-pack of books, or a book and some software), many stores won't let you return those purchases — at least not for full credit.

Keep all your receipts for books and materials too. Know a store's poli-cy for getting a refund. Is it 7 days, 30 days or something else? Being aware of the rules ahead of time can save you lots of aggravation and money in the long run when you want to sell back materials, or get a refund.

* * *

Desperate undergraduate and graduate students sometimes resort to two options that I would never recommend: photocopying textbooks or skipping much-needed textbooks altogether.

You are legally allowed to copy small portions of a textbook, such as a few pages that have math problems or the study questions at the end of a chapter. In some instances, you can even copy one full chapter. But copy-ing entire textbooks is illegal, and violates various copyright laws. It's true that you may not get busted for the infraction, but why risk it?

At the other end of the spectrum, some students just try to wing it in class and tough it out for a semester without any textbooks, even when those books are vitally important to a course.

That's an ultra-risky strategy. Best-case scenario you might skate by — or even do well — just based on your notes or handouts from the professor.

Worst-case scenario, you might do poorly — or even fail the course — simply because you missed out on reading or studying too much important information that could only be gleaned from the book.

I understand what it's like to be virtually penniless in college. Really, I do.

But with the numerous options I've just outlined, there's no good excuse to break the law or to break your own academic stride.

If I were a dead-broke student and I couldn't get a book through any other means, I'd write down the table of contents of the required book (easy enough to do in class with a friend's book). Then I'd go get a different — yet similar — book on the same topic, covering the same material, to keep up with the subject matter. I'd get that "similar" book via one of two places: the library or OpenStax College's free e-books.

Surely these are better solutions compared to engaging in copyright infringement, and risking expulsion from college, or going a whole school term without any books.

So here's the bottom line: By reviewing the strategies covered in this chapter, there are ways for even the most cash-strapped student to get those textbooks and supplies that are necessary for college success.

PART II

HIDDEN COSTS

CHAPTER 7

STUDENT-GENERATED COSTS

Now that we've covered a slew of hefty upfront expenses that college students face, you might think most of the spending you'll need for higher education is over.

Sadly, that's far from reality.

A report in the Fiscal Times once estimated that the true cost of a four-year degree can reach *twice* the advertised sticker price.

Think about that for a moment. It sounds insane, but it's actually all-too-true: if you're not careful, college expenses can wind up being *two times* what schools say.

So let's address why it is that college costs can turn out to be *double* what they're advertised.

The published price of a college usually focuses on four categories: tuition, fees, room and board. Colleges that want to be even more transparent about costs will include the costs of books and supplies, travel and personal expenses.

But because so much hype is devoted to talking about tuition and fees in particular, students and parents tend to hone in primarily on this cluster of expenses.

However, simply tallying up the *upfront* costs of college — the tuition, fees, room and board — misses much of the whole picture. You're just seeing the tip of the iceberg.

What about everything that comes *prior* to college enrollment? Aren't real dollars being spent on everything from SAT and ACT exams to pre-college programs to help give students an admissions edge? Of course they are!

That doesn't even account for costly test prep courses and tutors, cross-country campus visits and road tours, as well as pricey college applications. (If you doubt how expensive *pre*-college life can be, or if you just want to know how to conquer those bills, check out *College Secrets for Teens*.)

And what about all the "hidden" costs of college that students incur along their four-year (or longer) journey to graduation? They are very real expenses too, as you'll see over the next two chapters.

To properly plan for and realistically examine college costs, you absolutely must view these expenses from three different vantage points. There are:

1. *Pre-college* expenses to consider;
2. *Upfront* college costs you must know about; and
3. *Hidden* college costs to take into account

In *College Secrets for Teens*, I teach you about all about *pre-college* expenses you might encounter and how to minimize them.

Thus far, in *College Secrets*, we've explored the *upfront* college costs. Now it's time to analyze the *hidden* costs of college.

You must understand the "hidden" costs of higher education. Even when colleges seemingly put it all out there — telling you every possible *upfront* expense you must pay — that's really only a fraction of the expenses of college life.

This is true for all institutions of every type: private and public, non-profit and for-profit, small liberal arts colleges and big research universities, two-year and four-year institutions, and more.

It's largely because of the *hidden* costs of college that a joint study by Citigroup and *Seventeen* magazine found that six out of 10 undergraduates (61%) say college life is more expensive than they anticipated.

Even colleges that let you have a payment plan, where you divide up all your total costs over the course of the academic year, aren't being as transparent as possible about college expenses.

For instance, let's assume a public or private school is $30,000 in total — for tuition, fees, room and board. And let's further assume that you're *paying* the full price, out of your pocket. (We know from the earlier discussion on tuition discounting that this isn't likely for most students; but stay with me for a moment, just for the sake of illustration.)

At $30,000 a year, a school with an installment plan might let you pay $3,000 per month over 10 months. Sounds reasonable, right?

Well, if you fall for this kind of logic, it's the same as believing a car salesman who tells you that a $30,000 car will "only cost you $300 a month."

What that salesman is referring to is the monthly car payment alone.

But what about gas, monthly car insurance, or oil changes and maintenance that need to be done on a regular basis? And did the salesman mention that $30,000 is the "base" price for that shiny new vehicle? Probably not initially, because he doesn't want you to focus on the fact that you'll be paying more — a lot more, in fact — for any "accessories" or "upgrades" you might want.

Naturally, all those things cost extra money.

Just like you'll pay ongoing expenses for the privilege of driving that new set of wheels, so too are there ongoing expenses associated with being a college student. So the "upfront" costs we've covered are just one category of bills. There are a lot more.

Now, don't hit the "Panic" button just yet! Nor do I want you to fall out of your chair thinking that college is *truly* going to drive you into bankruptcy.

The good news is that even though the *real, total* cost of going to college is typically *far more expensive* than most colleges let on, that doesn't mean that *you will* have to shell out all those funds. Remember: *College Secrets* is designed to help you spend *less*, not more money.

So this chapter and the one that follows give you insights into "hidden" college costs that you won't find in any university viewbook or fancy college brochure. In fact, even college financial aid officers, as helpful as they might be, don't give you this information.

The "hidden" expenses I'll now reveal to you can be broken into four categories:

- Expenses generated by the student, primarily based on lifestyle and personal choices
- Expenses generated by the college or university, mainly as revenue generators

- Hybrid expenses that are a mixture of both student generated and school generated costs
- Miscellaneous or oddball expenses that defy pure categorization, and that can come out of left field, throwing a monkey wrench in your budget if you're not aware of them.

Suzanna De Baca is a vice president of wealth strategies at Ameriprise Financial, where the typical client is an affluent individual with $250,000 to $1 million in investable assets. Even with clients that have sizeable amounts of cash on hand, she finds that college costs can still catch some parents unaware.

"The Number 1 financial mistake people make in planning for college is not starting to save soon enough," says DeBaca. "The second biggest mistake is underestimating the true total cost of college."

Here's a quick overview of the student-generated costs typical for many undergraduate and graduate students:

- Car expenses
- Credit card bills and loans
- Clothing/wardrobe
- Dorm furnishings and decorations
- Eating out
- Electronics
- Extracurricular activities, hobbies and socializing
- Laundry
- Moving expenses
- Personal costs and miscellaneous spending
- Phone bills
- Summer months (2 to 3 months)
- Travel to and from home
- Tutoring

Like I said, don't panic just yet! You've made it this far. So you can certainly figure out a way to manage all of these costs, too.

And that's precisely what I'm about to tell you how to do.

Car Expenses

If you're thinking about having a car when you're on campus, you should think long and hard about the financial consequences of that choice. For many students, having a car while attending college is mostly just a money-drainer.

AAA reports that it costs nearly $8,900 annually to own and operate an average-sized sedan that's driven 15,000 miles a year. If you drive a small car just 10,000 miles annually, your yearly vehicle expenses drop to about $6,000. Even on the low end, that still works out to $500 a month just for the privilege of having a set of wheels at your disposal.

AAA's figures include operating costs, such as gas, maintenance and tires. The numbers also take into account ownership costs, like depreciation, insurance, license, registration and taxes. If you're financing a vehicle, realize that your car note comes *on top of* the $500 in car costs you'll be shelling out each month.

Parents who want to buy their teens a brand new car as a high school graduation or going-away-to-college gift should keep this financial reality in mind.

Remember how I previously suggested that it would be foolish to believe the car salesman who tells you that a new $30,000 vehicle will "only" cost you the $300 a month car payment? Well, this is why I made that assertion, and the experts from AAA agree with me.

"The true cost of vehicle ownership involves more than the sticker price and what you pay at the pump," says John Nielsen, AAA Managing Director of Automotive Engineering and Repair. "Before you make any vehicle purchase, it is important to determine ownership and operational costs and compare them to your current and future financial situation."

To help you figure out your individual driving costs, AAA has a Your Driving Costs brochure that contains a handy worksheet you can fill out using your specific area, driver and vehicle information.

Fortunately, if you decide to forgo having a car while you're at college, you have lots of good transportation options during your college years.

You can take public transportation. Most municipalities and schools give discounts to students buying local transportation passes. On very large campuses that are spread out, like Emory University or UC

Berkeley, school-provided transportation is free or included as part of your student fees.

You can also use Zipcar and UhaulCarShare, two popular car-sharing services that serve the college market. With rates as low as $5 an hour plus mileage, if you only need a car a couple times a month, getting a car from either one of these services will run you just $40 to $50 or so monthly. You can also hitch a ride with friends if you and your classmates just need to go to a local store, grab a bite at a nearby restaurant or venture out further away from campus for some reason.

From a financial perspective, all of these alternatives are far better than having your own car at college because you won't have the added cost of insurance, maintenance and constantly fueling up at the pump. Dumping your own car also means you won't have to deal with the hassles, and added expense, of parking on campus.

U.S. News and World Report recently created a list of national universities with the most cars on campus. At these institutions, many of which are commuter schools, 90% or more of the student body use a vehicle to get to school.

Out of the 178 universities that reported the car-specific data to *U.S. News*, nearly half (48%) of students had cars on campus. Some schools, however, had no student cars on campus. Among them: Georgetown University, Polytechnic Institute of New York University, and the University of Wisconsin, Madison.

Because so many students want to take their cars to college, it's created something of a parking crisis at many schools. So be sure to ask campus officials about any programs or initiatives they have to help students without cars. Such programs are becoming more and more common.

For instance, the University of New England provides free bikes to students who leave their cars at home. At the University of Wisconsin-Madison, 22% of students bike to school in good weather, thanks to the campus installing more bike racks, subsidizing membership in the city's bike-share program, and making investments in on-campus bike repair services.

Encouraging bicycling is one major way that schools nationwide are trying to decrease students' reliance on their vehicles. Other efforts are afoot too.

According to a recent U.S. PIRG study, colleges and universities are also increasingly supporting:

- The development of new walking paths
- Fare-free and discounted access to transit services
- Ride-sharing initiatives, such as carpooling
- Car-sharing programs
- Distance learning and online resources

If none of these strategies work for you, and you absolutely *must* have a car — or you're about to buy one before heading off to college —opt for a fuel-efficient vehicle, not a gas-guzzler. It will dramatically cut your gas costs.

* * *

You should also ask your auto insurance company about any discounts you may qualify for if your vehicle is mostly parked on campus and only driven a low number of miles.

To get the best deals on coverage, go to AutoInsurance.com, where you can comparison shop for auto insurance, buy it instantly, and save money all at the same time. Unlike other insurance-related websites, AutoInsurance.com isn't a lead generator that sells your information, and then you wind up later getting a ton of phone calls or emails from companies trying to solicit your business.

Instead, when you visit AutoInsurance.com, you simply enter your name, address, date of birth and contact information. Then you can opt-in to have the site pull your *existing* auto insurance policy. AutoInsurance.com is able to match up your current policy with bids from other auto insurance carriers. That way you can be sure you're comparing apples-to-apples in terms of coverage amounts and deductibles.

AutoInsurance.com offers you binding auto insurance quotes right on the spot from multiple insurers, including such top-rated companies as Progressive, Esurance, 21st Century, Travelers and others. In just a few minutes, you can see whether or not your existing policy is competitively priced — or whether you could get a much better deal by taking your business elsewhere.

Many people aren't aware of this: but if you find more affordable auto insurance coverage elsewhere, you don't have to stay locked in to your current insurer. You can simply cancel your auto insurance policy without penalty, and you'll get a refund for the unused amount.

Since AutoInsurance.com is a relatively new company, which started in 2014, you may not have heard of it until now. But you've no doubt heard of its partner: Walmart, which is the exclusive retail and marketing partner for AutoInsurance.com. Due to that affiliation, anyone can get online at Walmart.com or even go into Walmart stores to learn more about getting better auto insurance rates.

Credit Card Bills

For many students living on their own at college, credit cards have become a way of life.

Credit cards aren't inherently bad. You just have to know how to manage credit and debt wisely. You also have to realize that if you carry a balance, or make minimum payments, you'll be charged interest on top of the costs of the goods or services you purchased.

So let's talk about how young adults heading off to college can develop proper money habits and avoid excessive credit card debt.

Here are some credit card do's and don'ts for parents and their college-bound sons and daughters.

DO consider making the student an authorized user of the parent's card

Although federal laws now restrict credit card marketing on campuses, students can still be inundated by offers from banks and credit card companies. For many students, it's tempting to sign up for the first credit card offer that comes along, or even multiple cards, to cover personal and educational expenses in a pinch.

But for teens and young adults without proper budgeting know-how, or those who have never handled a credit card on their own, it may be better to start them off as an authorized user on a parent's credit card. This will allow the parent to monitor the student's spending and keep him or her accountable for any purchases made using that card.

DO weigh the pros and cons of having the student use a debit card

If you're a parent and you don't want your child linked to your credit accounts, or you're concerned about his money-management skills, suggest that he get a debit card that he can use to pay his bills.

It's a good way to help students effectively manage their money without worrying about the hassles of writing checks for day-to-day purchases.

Still, students do need to keep track of how they use their debit cards, either by keeping a running total of their card usage or regularly reviewing their online statements. Debit card users can also set up email alerts as notifications when their balance runs low. This is a smart idea because you don't want to use the card when there's not enough money in the account to cover your spending. If you do, you may get hit with overdraft fees or other bank charges.

DO consider the benefits of secured cards

If you're a college student and you want to establish a credit history during your college years, one way to achieve this goal is by applying for a secured credit card. You can manage that account on your own, or you can become a joint account holder with a parent.

Just like traditional unsecured credit cards, secured credit cards help people build credit by reporting one's payment history to the credit bureaus (Equifax, Experian and TransUnion). But secured cards differ from regular, unsecured cards in one significant way. Secured cards require a security deposit, which then becomes the credit line.

For example, if you put $500 on deposit with a bank, that bank can provide you (or your child) with a secured card that has a $500 credit limit. Parents who are co-users of their child's secured card would have access to that account, but could choose not to use it.

DON'T apply for several cards at a time

College students ready for a credit card should be selective in choosing which cards to apply for, to avoid hurting their credit scores. All credit card applications show up as hard inquiries on a credit report. Too many inquiries drag down your credit score, since inquiries stay on your credit report for two years, and they count against you — for the purpose of calculating your FICO credit score — for one year.

DON'T overlook student credit cards

If you think you (or your child) can be responsible enough to handle a credit card, by using it only when appropriate and/or paying off credit card balances before the end of each month, then consider the benefits of a student credit card. These cards offer rewards such as cash back on certain types of purchases, or airline miles and discounts to get you back home for the holidays, or to cut travel costs during spring break and other time periods.

In a recent credit card rewards study of the Best Credit Cards for Graduates (including high school and college grads), Cardhub selected the Journey Student Rewards Card from Capital One as its top pick for ongoing rewards.

Editors at Cardhub noted that the Journey Card offers 1% cash back across all purchases, a 25% cash back bonus when you pay your bill on time, and no annual fee.

They're great benefits. But what I like most about the Journey Card is that it also offers numerous other perks designed to promote financial literacy, boost credit education and encourage proper spending among young adults.

For example, students with a Journey Card can get free credit scores and also access Capital One's Credit Tracker tool at no cost.

Credit Tracker — which is available online and via a mobile app — contains a variety of bells and whistles that let students understand how their own financial behaviors impact their credit score.

For instance, the simulator on Credit Tracker is highly sophisticated, letting you see — among other things — what would happen to your credit score if you paid off all or a portion of your credit card debt, missed a payment, opened a new line of credit, or applied for a loan.

The simulator also allows you to envision potential progress over time, by showing you where your credit score would be in, say, 6 months, if you gradually paid off your credit card bills or simply made all your payments promptly during that time.

Other features of the interactive Credit Tracker tool include:

- A credit bureau summary
- A report card with letter grades, which shows six key factors (both positive and negative) influencing a person's credit score; and
- Credit bureau monitoring that gives students electronic, real-time alerts when anything important in their credit report changes, such as an inquiry for new credit or a new address suddenly being reported (a potential sign of identity theft)

All students should strive to maintain good credit. That's especially true for those completing their studies and entering the workforce, since employers are increasingly using credit checks as a way to screen job applicants.

While I think the Journey Card is a terrific option for students, whatever card you choose, just make sure to read the fine print for information about annual fees, interest rates and other terms.

DON'T forget to set specific guidelines and spending limits

Whether or not a parent adds a child to a credit account or the student applies for a separate credit card, it's important for families to discuss the prudent use of credit and when credit cards *shouldn't* be used.

It's far too easy to lose track of money spent while in college, with tuition bills each year — not to mention books, supplies, food and other expenses.

Parents should create realistic spending limits and urge their children to stick to those limits. Also, recommend that your child avoid using credit cards for routine day-to-day purchases that could easily be paid for with cash. Ditto for big-ticket items that he or she may not be able to pay off within the month.

Similarly, if you want your child to use the credit card for emergencies only, say so.

Despite the high credit card bills often racked up by college students, those four years spent earning a degree don't have to burden them with unmanageable debt.

If you follow the six do's and don'ts listed above, students can learn life-long money-management skills and keep credit card debt to a minimum — even while they're pursuing a higher education.

* * *

By the way, I can still remember when I got my first credit card. It was the 1986-1987 school year and I was a freshman at the University of California, Irvine.

What I recall most is walking into my dorm room for the first time, and finding applications for credit cards lying right there on my dorm bed. The mattress was completely bare, except for those credit card offers emblazoned with Visa and MasterCard logos.

To me, they were like formal invitations to adulthood. And sure enough, I later felt so grown up — *"I'm officially an adult!"* I thought — when I got approved for one, and then another and yet another of those nice, shiny pieces of plastic.

Too bad nobody taught me how to use credit wisely, how to budget, or even how to know when — and when not — to use my cards. (One good rule: emergency use of credit cards is OK; everyday use for pizza or clothes, not so much).

These days, the rules are different regarding credit cards for college kids. Because of the Credit Card Reform Act of 2009, credit card firms face restrictions in marketing credit cards to students.

If you're 21 or under, a parent must co-sign your credit card application; otherwise, you have to show enough income to be able to repay any credit card debt you incur.

It's OK to Have Credit Cards While in College

Despite the push to regulate credit cards for young adults, you shouldn't buy into the concept that credit cards are evil or *always* bad for college students.

On the contrary, when you're in the college phase of your life, and are preparing for the real world, a student credit card could be a key tool to help you start learning important financial concepts: things like budgeting, managing cash flow, and delayed gratification.

If you can get off to a good start with credit as a college student, hopefully you'll learn positive fiscal habits that will last a lifetime.

Clothing/Wardrobe

The most recent data from the National Retail Federation (NRF) show that college shoppers spend about $46 billion a year on apparel, supplies, dorm furnishings and more. On average, U.S. students and their parents dole out $837 on college purchases. The biggest collective chunk of that money, $232, went toward clothing, shoes and collegiate gear.

During your college years, you should think more like a budgetnista, instead of a fashionista, when it comes to buying clothing and making wardrobe choices.

Unfortunately, some students act like college is a four-year fashion show. For lots of teenagers going into college, back-to-school shopping is a time to load up on designer clothes and the latest trendy fashions. Even those students who aren't into brand-name labels nonetheless want to walk around campus wearing their school colors or clothing with college names and insignias.

But someone has to be an adult when it comes to clothing and set limits on wardrobe purchases.

If students won't do it, it's the job of responsible parents to rein in their children and emphasize price and quality over brand names and an obsession with the season's styles.

According to Capital One's 13th Annual Back-to-School Shopping Survey, nearly half of all parents surveyed (47%) consider price to be the most important factor when making a back-to-school purchase followed by quality (36%).

But for teens, only 22% of those surveyed consider price a top priority, and even fewer teens (10%) see quality as their biggest concern.

Among teenagers, nearly half of those surveyed (46%) said style and appearance top their priority list when making a back-to-school purchase.

One in five teens (19%) say brand names are the most important factor to consider when making purchases. (As one cool **infographic** has shown, clearly there's a big disconnect between teens and parents when it comes to style vs. price.)

As adults, we all know that fashions and styles can come and go. So help your 18-year-old understand that price really does matter, and that if they're wearing a pair of jeans or a sweater from last season — or even, *heaven forbid*, a year or two ago — that's perfectly fine.

Also remember the importance of comparison-shopping for clothes and other school merchandise.

Sites like Dealnews.com are good for alerting you to sales, promotions, coupons, rebates and other ways to save money during the back-to-school season.

A bit of other advice to parents: Whether you're shopping in stores or online, let your children know that you value discounts and getting a good deal. One way you can do that is by comparison shopping together — and letting your son or daughter join the hunt for the best deal.

It's not only more fun when you make bargain-hunting a family affair, you're also imparting two important financial lessons: that saving money is important, and that high prices don't always equal the best or most desirable merchandise.

Don't feel compelled to buy everything your son or daughter asks for or even claims to need during the back-to-school season. The reality is that some purchases can wait — especially things that your kids simply *want* and don't really need.

Get comfortable saying "No" to those extra items and non-essential goods that may be discounted later, during the holiday season a few months down the road.

The purpose of pulling back on some spending isn't to be a Scrooge. It's to help teach your children about wants versus needs. Teaching them to wait to get some items will help them curb impulse spending and learn to practice delayed gratification.

These are skills that will aid your children not just during back-to-school season, but over the course of their lifetime.

Dorm Furnishings and Decorations

The NRF's Back to College survey reveals that spending on dorm and apartment furnishings is on the rise. Two in five (42%) families spent an average $105 on new bedding, small refrigerators and microwaves.

For some families, that figure may be way too high, and for others it could be far too low.

That's why parents need to talk to their teenagers and college-age students about creating a realistic back-to-school shopping budget based on your family's circumstances.

The goal should be to determine a pre-set spending limit that you both agree to — and you do it *before* you go shopping. That way, you establish expectations and your kid learns to live within his or her means.

As for other ways to save money on dorm furnishings, don't buy everything new. Look for used appliances that are in good condition. You can get them from local yard sales or off eBay or Craigslist.

You should even consider skipping on some items altogether. Students can connect with their roommates before school begins and coordinate who will bring what items. There's no point in having two mini-fridges or multiple microwaves in a dorm room. So just have one student bring one of those items; the other roommate can bring another appliance.

Eating Out

The average student spends about $765 to dine off-campus, according to Student Monitor. It's all too easy to overspend when many restaurants and eateries in college areas let students pay just by swiping their school ID cards.

There's another reason students fork over a lot of dollars eating out: it's their first time away from home and mom and dad aren't around to serve those nice home-cooked meals. So in place of ready-made meals, many college students turn to fast food outlets, pizza shops (either takeout or delivery) and other restaurants of choice.

It may seem like just $5 here or $10 there, but frequent eating out really adds up over time. Just $20 a week in dining expenses can put you at $760 in restaurant spending over the course of a nine-month school year.

Obviously, if you eat out more frequently while in college, or prefer pricier food joints, that spending tally can surge even more dramatically.

Instead of eating out all the time, make good use of your campus meal plan if you have one. Alternatively, make weekly trips to the grocery store for healthy snacks and food. Cooking your own meals can save a lot of money over time.

Limit dining out to special occasions or once-in-a-blue-moon type of events. When you do eat out, favor local restaurants that give you nice student discounts off your bill. Some daily deal websites, like Moocho. com, will also alert you to special restaurant promotions, such as half-off deals for students. Chegg's Campus Deals, which acquired and rebranded CampusSpecial.com in 2014, likewise lets students at more than 500 college campuses order and pay for food, as well as discover offers from local and national merchants. By the end of 2015, Chegg expects its Campus Deals platform to be available for more than 1,000 U.S. colleges.

Electronics

Besides the clothing, shoes and collegiate gear category, the next largest portion of college shoppers' budgets is spent on electronics — about $203 annually according to NRF data.

About 60% of students buy a new computer, MP3 player, smart phone or other device. If you go all out, and get a new flat screen TV or other electronics for a dorm room, your costs can quickly skyrocket.

As with all college spending, don't splurge on the unnecessary stuff. Refrain from buying items that simply cater to lifestyle preferences but aren't really essential to college life. Don't try to impress roommates and others with the latest gadgets and tech toys — even if they are "cool" and fun. One problem with keeping up with the Joneses is that the cycle of spending can never end, putting a serious dent in your budget and your long-term financial security.

Do I really need to say that it's probably a bad financial decision if you find yourself regularly standing in hour-long lines at the cell phone store, trying to get your service reconnected as you peruse the latest, greatest model of the "best next-generation" phone? You should just mail in your payments and forego the additional sales pressure to upgrade. Staying out of that cell phone store will also help you avoid unnecessary temptations to buy yet another cell phone.

If you have to purchase a new computer or laptop, comparison shop and use sites like TigerDirect.com, which regularly features liquidation sales from various merchants and retailers. Look for deals and coupons on computer software too, which is frequently discounted up to 75% for students.

If you're a Mac computer lover or an Apple loyalist, you can save money by purchasing refurbished instead of a brand new Apple product.

If you need a new tablet, does it really have to be a Mac product? How about a $38 tablet that's all the rage? You might check out the new UbiSlate 7Ci from DataWind and decide that it's not for you. Then again, you may fall in love with it.

Either way, at least you know that this low-cost 7-inch Android tablet exists and that it's about 15 times less than the latest Apple iPad or Samsung Galaxy Note. In fact, for those on a tight budget, the UbiSlate tablet also happens to currently be the least expensive tablet computer in the United States.

One final tip regarding electronics — retailers typically try to sell you extended warranty protection when you are buying electronic gadgets, computers, and appliances. Do your homework before you shop. You may already have an adequate warranty from the manufacturer and the credit card that you choose to use may already give you an extended warranty. If so, pass on a retailer's warranty offer.

Extracurricular Activities, Hobbies and Socializing

When socializing with friends in college, try to make social events center around free activities, like visiting museums or just hanging out together in dorm halls — as opposed to doing things that cost money, like going shopping, going out to the movies or going out eating. With all that going, going, going, your money will also be going — out of your wallet!

Some extracurricular activities and hobbies that students want to pursue in college are free, but others rack up big bills. If you want to be on the cheer team at San Diego State University, hoorah for you! But it'll cost you $600 a year.

Outdoor activities that take advantage of local or national parks, municipal sites, and other government attractions often fall into the free or low-cost categories. Those are real budget-savers. They can also get you outside, and help keep you from feeling too cooped up when you've been in a dorm room or classroom way too long.

When choosing hobbies, favor those that require your time, creativity and knowledge — as opposed to your money, special equipment or costly gear.

Also, don't buy a ton of gear upfront — especially when you're just learning a new skill or getting into a hobby for the first time. If you need gear when you're a novice, rent it. There's no point in going all out and buying expensive golf clubs, high-tech camera equipment, or costly ski gear if you're not going to regularly use those items.

You may take an initial interest in golf, photography or skiing, and then decide after one season or so that you're not that into it any more. Save yourself money by forgoing upfront purchases for such hobbies and extra-curricular activities.

As a final way to save cash, consider taking on hobbies that can slash your costs in other ways. For instance, if you get into biking as an exercise pastime, can you envision yourself giving up your car and lowering auto expenses? Or what about those who love arts and crafts? If you enjoy woodworking, painting or cooking, you may be able to make gifts for others — and not have to spend money on store-bought gifts for your loved ones when holidays, birthdays or other special occasions roll around.

Laundry

One of the perks of living at home is that Mom or Dad usually does the laundry. That's not the case, however, if you're a college student far away from your parents. For better or worse, when you're getting your four-year degree, it's mostly up to you to handle your laundry.

Doing laundry on your own doesn't just take time out of your schedule; it also takes money. Whether you clean your clothes on campus or go off-campus to a local laundromat, expect to pay about $2 to $3 a load to wash and dry your clothes. That may seem ultra cheap, but doing the equivalent of two loads a week at $3 a load will cost you more than $200 during the school year.

Fortunately, some schools are now including laundry services as part of their tuition and fees. You just swipe your campus ID card, or a special card given to you for laundry use, and use the on-campus laundry facilities to clean your own clothes. Other schools make you use coin-operated machines to do the laundry.

One exception to this practice is Davidson College, a private liberal arts school in North Carolina. At Davidson, students simply drop off their clothes in bags at an on-campus laundry center. A day or two later, the clothes get returned to them cleaned and even folded. That sweet perk is going away, however. Starting in May 2015, students at Davidson will have to do their own laundry. The change will save the school about $400,000 a year.

* * *

You can also sometimes find cheap off-campus laundry services, like MyLazyBones, which will come to your college once a week, pick up your clothes, and do the laundry for you — at prices that vary based on the region or campus. Be sure to check around for the best local rates. Some laundry operators serving colleges and universities charge students as much as $1,000 per academic year for this service.

You can save on overall laundry costs by wearing jeans, sweatpants and other clothing that doesn't have to be washed after a single use. Also, pay attention to your activities. Are you the kind of guy who'll be playing football games on the lawn almost daily with your buddies, eating pizza for breakfast, lunch and dinner, or partaking in pie-eating contests? If so, pretty much all of those things can virtually guarantee that your laundry bills will be higher.

When you wash your dirty clothes, don't waste money on expensive detergents and other costly laundry cleaning aids. Off-brand products will clean your clothes just fine, as will most bleach solutions — even if they're not products whose names you recognize.

Fabric softeners are other culprits adding to the cost of laundry. Fabric softeners can run $3 to $7 per container, depending on the brand you select and in which part of the country you live. So try doing some loads of laundry without a softener and see if you really miss it. If you desperately need that fragrant scent, you can always go ahead and buy a low-cost product later. In the meantime, you might just discover that your clothes are fresh and clean without the added boost of a fabric softener.

Moving Expenses

The transition from home to college can generate bills in and of itself if you plan on using a moving service to haul lots of stuff to your college dorm or apartment. Ditch that idea. Instead, use the family car when possible. Send stuff ahead to avoid baggage fees if you'll be flying, and know that sometimes less truly is more.

If you're moving a long distance, realize too that there are some things you can buy once you arrive at your travel destination. You don't want to load up your car with a bunch of unnecessary items if you're planning a long road trip to get you to college.

By de-cluttering and lightening the load in your car, you'll spend less money on gas and increase your vehicle's fuel efficiency along the way.

Personal Costs and Miscellaneous Spending

Are you (or is your child) a big spender? Maybe you're a young lady who likes to get her hair and nails done all the time, or who hoards tons of makeup, lotion and cosmetics. If so, watch out for these spending traits. Such lifestyle expenses can easily spiral out of control if not properly managed, especially the first year or two of college.

To keep personal costs down and miscellaneous spending to a minimum, follow a few budgeting tips.

Here's my simple two-step process for creating a basic budget. It's fast, easy, and anyone can do it.

Step 1: Itemize ALL of Your Expenses

Create a list of everything you spend money on — whether those expenditures are weekly, monthly, or yearly. Use different categories to group all your expenses.

Examples of common budget categories include:

- Credit card payments
- Educational costs or student loans
- Entertainment
- Food
- Housing
- Insurance
- Miscellaneous
- Savings
- Transportation
- Utilities

Obviously, some of these categories may not apply to you. Use whatever is relevant or add additional categories that describe your own spending. Be thorough!

Don't forget about annual memberships, magazine subscriptions, books, or money spent on gifts for birthdays, graduations, holidays, and special occasions. Your list can be written down or entered on a computer spreadsheet.

Step 2: Adjust to Avoid Budget-Wreckers

If your expenses exceed your income (i.e. money from a job, funds you get from your parents, and scholarships/grants awarded to you), you'll have to cut back in areas that aren't necessities.

Stop going out to eat. Say goodbye (temporarily at least) to that premium cable TV package. Forgo shopping trips to the mall. You get the point.

After you quit making luxury purchases or spending money on things that aren't absolute necessities, if your expenses still surpass your income, you'll have to make additional adjustments to your budget — this time slimming down on those "necessities."

You should also adjust your budget to plan for and/or avoid the common budget-wreckers that everyone faces — things like emergencies that pop up from time to time.

Don't ever think: "There's no place else I can cut my budget!"

I hear this lament all the time, and invariably I'm able to show people places in their budget where they do have some flexibility — if they choose to make deeper cuts.

While you're adjusting your budget to match up your spending and income, the goal is to first get your expenses down so that they're less than your take-home income.

Then you want to create enough cash flow so that you have some money left over at the end of the month — and you're not merely living like a total pauper or going paycheck to paycheck without getting ahead. Over time, if you stick to your budget, you'll get to the point where you'll have positive cash flow, and start building savings.

It's important to realize, however, that spending on personal items isn't the only way you might ruin your budget at school.

Some students complain that dorm bathrooms can be gross or that their roommates are total slobs. Even if you're just buying products for your dorm or apartment, beware of the risk of overspending to address these problems.

For instance, consider all the fancy household cleaners you might be buying: foaming bleach cleansers; special toilet bowl aides; or maybe high-priced furniture-cleaning solutions. Most things in your dorm, apartment or residence hall can be cleaned very well with a simple soap and water mix, or a touch of vinegar or ammonia added to the mix.

I like a sparkling, fresh-smelling bath or kitchen just as much as the next person. But you also need to make sure you're not getting sucked into buying cleaning products just because they have a good marketing pitch. If you're in a higher-end residence and have new items like leather sofas or freshly installed granite countertops, just read the care label first so you don't damage them.

You can also use cotton rags or reusable cloths for spills and to clean your countertops and tables. Paper towels are just a convenience — and an expensive one at that. Think about it this way: Do they use paper towels to clean up in restaurants? Of course not, because it would cost them a small fortune. Think the same way and save yourself money year-round by passing on those paper towels while in college.

Phone Bills

Most college students have cell phones as opposed to landlines. But some students have both. Either way, those phone lines don't come free. According to a study conducted recently by Cowen and Company, American consumers pay more for wireless phone service than consumers in any other country in the world.

Among the four major mobile carriers in the United States, Verizon is the most expensive of the bunch, with bills averaging $148 per month including taxes and fees. Sprint has the second most expensive service at an average monthly cost of $144. AT&T is the third priciest among wireless providers, with an average monthly charge of $141. And T-Mobile has the cheapest service, averaging $120 per month.

Those figures include both single users and family plan customers. The report didn't break out the average cost for an individual cell phone customer. But other studies have put that cost at about $70 monthly.

It may come as no surprise, but most college students aren't footing those hefty bills.

Citigroup's college spending survey showed that 60% of students say their parents pay their cell phone bills; only 35% of students paid for their own cell phone accounts.

Regardless of who's paying the tab, you can slash your cell phone bills. Here's how.

End "Wireless Waste"

A mobile phone analytics company called Validas is on a mission to eliminate so-called "wireless waste" — unused minutes, data and texts.

Validas makes its money by performing analysis of cell phone usage for large corporations. But it recently launched an initiative called SaveLoveGive.com to provide the same service for free to individuals.

Validas says that 80% of Americans overspend by an average of $200 annually. By seeing where you may be wasting cell phone usage, you can switch to a plan that better fits your actual needs, saving you money.

Claim Your Phone Discount

Many people are eligible for phone discounts either when they sign up for new service or later when they're ongoing customers. But most consumers don't know about these benefits or they forget to take advantage of them.

You may qualify for a reduction in your phone bill if your employer or your parent's employer has negotiated a discount with a cell phone provider. Tens of thousands of corporations have such agreements in place. Teachers, government employees, AAA members, credit union members and students can qualify as well — netting 10% to 25% off their phone bills.

To find out if you can get these sweet deals, visit the discount pages at AT&T, Sprint, and Verizon and enter your email address or mobile number.

In February 2014, T-Mobile ended its Advantage discount program for new customers. The program had offered consumers 15% price breaks based on an individual's affiliation with various associations. T-Mobile customers with accounts that predate the early 2014 switch continue to enjoy their discounts. Those current T-Mobile customers can check the T-Mobile Advantage Program page for businesses to see if they qualify for a discount through their employer.

Dispute Questionable Fees and Hidden Phone Surcharges

If you check your phone bill regularly, and scrutinize all the charges, you'll likely see a lot of little charges, some of which you don't need and probably don't have to pay each month. Examples include charges for roadside assistance, 411 phone service, or other random fees like horoscope texts and questionable toll-numbers that you don't recognize. Whenever you see such fees, dispute them immediately. Otherwise, you'll get billed for them month after month, which is a waste of money.

Get Free Phone Service Compliments of the Federal Government

Finally, I'll bet you didn't know about a government benefit program called Lifeline that can help low-income individuals and families save money on costly phone bills.

Lifeline is a federal assistance program that provides discounts on monthly telephone service for eligible consumers. The goal is to ensure that low-income households have phone access to stay connected to various essentials, such as 911 service, family members, and job opportunities.

The federal Universal Service Fund supports Lifeline.

The Lifeline program helps low-income households get landline or wireless telephone service by providing discounts that average $9.25 a month on one basic phone service. In some states, the discounts can be higher.

Lifeline is available in every state in the U.S. as well as Washington D.C. and on Tribal lands and U.S. territories too.

Eligibility Criteria for Lifeline

In order to enroll in Lifeline, you must demonstrate your eligibility by showing proof of income or participation in a qualifying program.

To be eligible, your household income must be at or below 135% of the federal Poverty Guidelines.

Alternatively, you are deemed eligible for Lifeline if you participate in one of the following assistance programs:

- Medicaid;
- Supplemental Nutrition Assistance Program (Food Stamps or SNAP);
- Supplemental Security Income (SSI);
- Federal Public Housing Assistance (Section 8);
- Low-Income Home Energy Assistance Program (LIHEAP);
- Temporary Assistance to Needy Families (TANF);
- National School Lunch Program's Free Lunch Program;
- Bureau of Indian Affairs General Assistance;

- Tribally-Administered Temporary Assistance for Needy Families (TTANF);
- Food Distribution Program on Indian Reservations (FDPIR);
- Head Start (if income eligibility criteria are met); or
- State assistance programs (if applicable).

The Lifeline service is a non-transferable benefit. So it's important to realize that you can't transfer the service (or give your Lifeline-supported phone) to any other individual.

You may also have to re-certify annually that you are eligible for Lifeline.

Here's the information that the government will need when you sign up for Lifeline:

- Name and address information — If you don't have a permanent residential address, you must provide a temporary address, which cannot be a P.O. Box.
- If a you are living at a temporary address, the telephone service provider or state agency may require confirmation of the address;
- Date of birth;
- The last 4 digits of your Social Security Number

Once you get Lifeline, you must notify Lifeline within 30 days if you move, or if you are no longer eligible for the service.

To enroll in Lifeline, just apply through your local telephone company or designated state agency. To locate a Lifeline provider in your state go to: http://www.lifelinesupport.org.

For more information about Lifeline, visit the Universal Service Administrative Company's website, call USAC's toll-free number (1-888-641-8722), call the FCC's toll-free customer service number (1-888-CALL-FCC), or contact your local telephone company.

Summer Months

School isn't in session all year long. College students still have to live — sometimes on their own — for the two or three months while school's out. That costs money too. So plan accordingly for how you'll manage expenses over the summer months. Some students who won't be going back home may opt to simply stay on campus. Thankfully, many schools have discounted room and board rates over the summer.

Alternatively, students wanting a bit more independence might take up residence with a roommate or two in off-campus housing or nearby apartments during the summer. Look for landlords that will give you a short-term lease or a month-to-month contract. That way you'll avoid having to break a rental agreement, which can result in hefty fees.

Housing won't be your only cost during the summer. All the other expenses mentioned thus far may come into play. So work that into your annual budget following the budgeting tips offered earlier in this chapter. Needless to say, getting a part-time or full time job or a paid internship in the summer months is a great way to pay for your school or living expenses or possibly build up a bit of savings.

Travel to and From Home

How often students will want to come home from college will depend on a lot of factors: how near or far Mom and Dad's home is located from school, how much independence the student wants to establish, and even other priorities and activities going on in a student's life, such as work, sports or extra-curricular commitments.

But most students will come home at least once or twice a year, either during the November-December holidays or the summer. Others return home more frequently, for instance to visit their parents over Spring Break or during other down periods.

Whatever the case, you can save money getting home with things like a Student Advantage card or by taking advantage of discounts of up to 20% off travel offered to students by Amtrak and Greyhound bus company. It's a good idea to ask around campus — or even via your social networks — to find other college students or nearby friends who may be driving home when school lets out. You may be able to hitch a ride with one of them, splitting the gas costs or getting an entirely free ride home.

Don't forget too, that some travel costs may go the other way: when parents come to visit their college children. Unfortunately, many hotels jack up their rates during local college events known as Parents Week.

Websites like Zimride.com — which is operated by Enterprise, the car rental company — can help you find ride shares with other students and individuals who are going your way or heading from one destination to another. The Zimride service works by tapping social networks to enable real, in-person connections between drivers and passengers.

Tutoring

College students who want extra help in studying for tough subjects or prepping for exams could pay anywhere from $25 an hour to $200 an hour for private tutoring.

At tutoring charges of just $50 an hour for 10 hours in a semester, you'd be shelling out $500 per term, or $1,000 every school year.

To cut those costs, you can do a lot of things.

Form study groups with your classmates and go over course material together. Sit in on free online courses or workshops offered by your campus or other colleges and universities. And most of all, take advantage of the free tutoring offered on most college campuses. You're likely already paying for this in the form of your student fees or other charges on your college billing statement.

Sometimes free tutoring is offered through the specific department where you're majoring. At other times it may be provided via a Student Success Center or an on-campus Learning Center.

Studies show that students who receive tutoring are more successful than those who don't. And research from the Association for Supervision and Curriculum Development (ASCD) suggests that college students are increasingly in need of tutoring services. According to a report from the ASCD, 43% of students at public two-year institutions and 29% of those attending public four-year colleges said they were required to enroll in a remedial course. The report notes that those figures don't even include the roughly 1.2 million students who dropped out of college. Many of them no doubt had academic challenges as well.

So wherever you can find free tutoring help, go get it. And don't feel bad about wanting or needing such assistance, either. Your academic success may depend on it.

CHAPTER 8

$\mathcal{S}$CHOOL $\mathcal{G}$ENERATED, $\mathcal{H}$YBRID, AND $\mathcal{M}$ISCELLANEOUS $\mathcal{C}$OSTS

When college and university officials speak about their campuses, they do a good job of letting prospective students and families know about the range of academic offerings, extracurricular opportunities, student services and facilities at these institutions.

There's the snazzy new athletic center that was just built where you can work out — or just watch a game.

There's the convenient Student Services building where you can get tutoring or the massive library near the dorms, where you can burn the midnight oil and print out that lab report you need to submit for your Bio class.

And then there's the tempting array of student clubs and activities where you can develop your talents or satisfy just about any personal interests you have.

You can't go on a single campus tour or information session without learning about all the wonderful treasures that await you when you're a higher education student.

Do you want to study abroad? Check. They've got you covered.

Are you interested in joining a fraternity or sorority? Check. Most four-year schools have plenty.

Are you considering doing field research domestically or internationally? Check. Faculty would love to help you with that.

Or maybe you want to major in engineering and minor in art? Check. That's not a problem, either.

In the recruiting phase, schools officials boast about the "wealth of experiences and opportunities" you'll derive from college. They *should* proclaim these benefits because, for the most part, what they're saying is absolutely true.

But there's a gaping hole the size of Texas in this whole conversation about the "opportunities" available at college.

That missing element is the shocking lack of conversation about the *financial exchange* that is necessary to make all of these wonderful opportunities materialize. In short, here's what that *exchange* boils down to: you (the student or parents) must pay the school for a long list of things — some of which you'll use, some of which you won't — and in exchange the school will make its vast resources and experiences available to you. That is the reality of getting a four-year degree in America.

So why is it that, amid all the exciting conversations about the 200 student clubs on campus or the discussions about the school's wide-ranging facilities, money is rarely if ever mentioned?

In fact, to the extent that the subject of finances is raised at all, it's only in the context of a brief "financial aid" Q&A, or when students and parents get shuttled off to a 30-minute or so session with a financial aid counselor to learn about the rules of college financial aid. Invariably, money matters in these forums are relegated strictly to a school's *upfront* costs — tuition, fees, room and board, books and supplies. Schools with a bit more disclosure might mention how "families need to budget for extras" like a student's personal expenses, or travel back home. But that's pretty much it.

There is almost *never*, I repeat *never*, any discussion of what *hidden* costs you'll encounter in higher education, especially to take advantage of the "tremendous opportunities and activities" that a school lays at your feet and encourages you to partake in while you're a college student.

I've just shared with you, in the previous chapter, hidden college costs that are student-generated, based on lifestyle and personal choices. Some college officials might reasonably argue that those costs are on you. After all, you can make the choice whether to incur many of those expenses or not.

But the same can't be said of the expenses I'll relate in this chapter, which are primarily *school-generated* costs. These back-end fees, hidden expenses and questionable surcharges often surprise parents and students alike. The fees range from the superbly sneaky to the lame and laughable. They include administrative padding, high markups, and many costs that colleges charge for no other reason than because they can get away with it. Truthfully, most of these expenses are charges that you would expect to find at profit-making enterprises — even though most U.S. colleges and universities are, or claim to be, non-profits.

Most families don't find out about these hidden costs until they actually get charged for the bills. A tiny fraction of individuals may know about some of these expenses, if they spend any time hunting around on college websites. That's basically the only place you'll find most of these additional fees, and even then they're typically buried deep within some hard-to-find webpage.

For instance, if you want to know about fees at UCLA, there's a main Registrar's page about fees. This main "fees menu" page then links you to more than *four dozen* other pages, including Annual Fee Charts, Term Fee Charts, Housing Rates, Miscellaneous Fees, special Notices and Letters about fees, Fee Descriptions and more. It would literally take a student or parent hours upon hours (if not days) to pore through all of these, much less make sense out of everything.

It's a true disappointment that for most colleges, such disclosure becomes their first and last line of defense. It's their fallback position when questioned about hidden fees. They feel that they've done their job of disclosing the true cost of higher education if they've revealed, in the fine print of some online document, that you'll have to pay extra fees for study abroad, for printing that lab report, joining that sorority, or just to take an art class. That's to say nothing of the outrageous late-payment penalties or "sucker" fees you'll read about shortly.

I think it's totally disingenuous and one of the biggest financial travesties taking place in higher education.

Instead of being truly transparent and upfront with students and parents about a slew of expenses, colleges and universities hide the true costs of college and keep numerous fees in the shadows as a way to lure students and trick families into thinking that these institutions are "affordable" when many simply are not.

This financial chicanery helps explain, in part, why so many college graduates come out of school with tens of thousands of dollars in student loan debt. If people don't know all the real costs of getting an education, how can they adequately plan, prepare for and pay such expenses without borrowing?

A failure to candidly talk about true college costs and to divulge those expenses in an upfront, transparent way also contributes to the college dropout problem in America. Since about 60% of students who leave U.S. schools without a degree cite *financial reasons* as the main problem they faced, when are higher education administrators, staff and faculty going to take their share of responsibility for this issue?

Thus far, American colleges and universities have shown little to no inclination to help fix the problem of non-disclosure about college fees and costs. In fact, most of them are increasingly moving in the opposite direction of finding a true solution.

Instead of making fees more transparent, readily accessible and understandable, schools often mask fees in a variety of ways to diminish public outcry about the rising cost of a college education. One of the ways schools skillfully mask costs is by rolling a long list of fees into a single charge. This has the effect of silencing those protests that might erupt if students truly realized how much they were being nickel and dimed. But don't be fooled by such financial games. A fee is still a fee — even if it's bundled with other charges, buried in the fine print of a school's website, masked by accounting maneuvers, or simply renamed to make it sound more palatable to students and their families.

It's time to start a real conversation in America about what it truly costs, financially, to deliver a good college education and what prices schools must charge to do that. This would take away the whole charade surrounding schools granting tuition discounts, a process that baffles most families and leaves colleges and universities struggling to have a sustainable pricing model.

It's also high time that public institutions, in particular, stopped hiding behind "a lack of state funding" as the reason they impose all sorts of fees on students.

Even though private schools outnumber public institutions by about three to one in America, public colleges and universities nonetheless enroll about 70% of all degree-seekers. So they have a special role to play in fixing this mess. In their defense, it's true that public institutions get their revenues mainly from state funding and the tuition and fees that students pay. Unfortunately, since 2012, more than 40 states nationwide have been hit by reductions in state funding, leaving many officials at public colleges feeling that they have no choice than to make up revenue shortfalls from tuition and fees.

But why haven't public colleges and universities — which employ some of the best economists and thinkers on the planet — been able to come up with viable solutions to the problem of reduced state aid? We all know this is an issue; it's been that way for years and all available evidence suggests that this trend will continue. Is it fair then, or even *feasible*, for public school officials to think they can simply keep charging families ever-higher tuition and fees as a way to deal with shortages in state aid? Certainly not.

Some creative problem-solving is needed to come up with other solutions: whether it's a more cost-efficient delivery of education via online courses, fewer high paid professors and faculty members, or other viable options that involve the colleges themselves adjusting bloated costs, something has to be done. If schools don't make adjustments on their own, then they risk market forces doing it for them. Sooner or later, students will turn in increasing numbers to a range of other options — whether that's going overseas to study at much cheaper schools, passing on pricey schools in favor of more affordable ones, or simply choosing not to attend college at all. Futurist Thomas Frey even predicts that 50% of all colleges will fail by 2030. Harvard Business School professor Clayton Christensen has issued a similar forecast.

Whether those predictions come true remains to be seen. But the handwriting is on the wall. The question is: are colleges seeing the message clearly? If so, they should be willing to address these very real, very serious problems.

* * *

In the meantime, until meaningful changes happen, let's look at what you'll be facing when it comes to *hidden* colleges costs — and what you can do about those expenses.

School-Generated Expenses

As mentioned, there are a host of school-generated expenses you should know in advance in order to deal with the issue of hidden or "back-end" costs that are prevalent at most colleges and universities.

These expenses can be grouped into eight main categories:

Course materials and other requirements for various majors
Credit for prior learning
Graduation fees
One-time fees
Parking fees
Printing fees
Tuition differential or surcharges for certain majors
Tuition inflation

What follows is an explanation of these fees and expenses, as well as strategies to reduce or avoid these surcharges. They're the kind of costs that school officials never talk about — but nonetheless expect you to pay once you've enrolled in school.

Course Materials and Other Requirements for Various Majors

Do you plan on taking classes like art, photography, journalism or broadcasting? Maybe you're planning to major in TV and film studies, or engineering. If so, be aware of all the extras large and small you'll pay for, including course materials and other requirements in these and similar majors.

Photography students may be required to buy certain cameras, to purchase film or to go out on costly photo shoots that they pay for out of pocket. Likewise, students in broadcasting often rent expensive hi-definition video cameras, tripods, and other equipment necessary to create news stories or visual projects.

Many students mistakenly think that at least the basic materials you need for certain courses are baked into the price of tuition and fees. But that's not the case at all with classes that rely heavily on your use of certain materials. Art students, for example, may have to routinely purchase paints, oils, canvases or posters, brushes, special pens and other utensils. In addition, those same art students typically pay an art studio fee, and art model fee and an art practicum fee (each about $50 to $150) per course.

To save money on course materials, you should look into sharing with classmates and splitting the costs for supplies. Many students even ask their professors for supplies. Often they'll have extra materials, items they're not using, or things they'd be happy to loan. You should also save any materials you purchase and treat them with care. That way, you prolong the life of those items and may be able to get use out of them in the next semester or even the next year.

Credit for Prior Learning

Sure, you shaved college costs by taking classes elsewhere, or testing out of an intro college class via AP exams or CLEP, the College Level Examination Program. But that doesn't mean colleges and universities let you off the hook financially for this advanced work. Many institutions charge you a fee just for your prior learning. This fee will often be labeled a "prior learning" charge or a prior learning "assessment." Recently, at Concordia University Chicago, their charge for prior learning was $235 per topic. Some two-year and four-year schools also have a similar fee imposed for giving you "work experience credit." These fees are a huge money-grab. Even if they have to "assess" your prior knowledge, it certainly doesn't cost hundreds of dollars for them to do that.

If you've taken AP or CLEP exams, you no doubt want the college credit for them. And you should get it. So to reduce these fees for prior learning, inquire about any waivers your school may offer. If it would be a hardship for you to pay those fees, you can also write to a school official requesting an appeal or special consideration to have those charges removed. Students who took AP exams free of charge or at a reduced cost, based on their low-income status or other eligibility factors, will likely have the greatest success in making the argument for a fee waiver at their colleges and universities. For any fee you might consider contesting or seeking a waiver for, see if your school has a "Petition for Special Consideration" form or similar process.

Graduation Fees

Picture this: You're now a senior in college and you've worked very hard to earn your four-year degree. You've probably pulled all-nighters and pushed yourself in ways you didn't know you could. Graduation time is finally here. Now you just want to celebrate and breathe a sigh of relief — especially if you've navigated all the litany of college costs thrown at you up to this point.

Well, take a deep breath, and get ready to open your wallet once more, because there are still more fees as you go out the door and bid your college or university farewell. Yes, you get charged just to graduate.

Graduation fees are typically $50 to $100, but they can be all over the place. They run from a low of $25 at schools like the University of Idaho to a high of $200 at campuses like John Carroll University, which also hits you with a $125 late fee if you don't pay your graduation fee on time.

Schools that impose a "graduation fee" say they do so for a variety of legitimate reasons. But many students feel like the fee is just an exit tax of sorts.

Many colleges and universities impose a graduation fee for the academic apparel they provide you — like the cap, gown and tassel you'll wear on graduation day. Other schools levy the graduation fee as an administrative cost to "cover" the expense of creating, printing and mailing you your long-awaited diploma. Some schools impose a graduation fee as a mix of both. For instance, at Humboldt State University in Humboldt, CA, the school's $58 graduation fee includes a $33 charge for "commencement" as well as a $25 charge for "the diploma/degree check." I guess it costs $25 for someone to perform three or four clicks on a computer, check your academic records online, and see whether or not your GPA is adequate and you've earned all the credits necessary to graduate.

Not all schools charge "graduation" fees — at least not officially. At UC Berkeley, for example, there reportedly aren't any graduation fees, but the university does charge $10 a pop for commencement tickets. (And yes, graduates must pay for a ticket, too).

Upon closer inspection, however, you'll find that Berkeley consolidated 11 fees — including eliminating some fees too — back in 2011. Like other UC campuses, Berkeley now charges undergraduates a "Document

Management Fee." Berkeley's Document Management Fee is $172 and covers a host of things, including "unlimited official transcripts" and "one diploma mailed at no charge using standard shipping." I'm not sure how school officials can charge you a fee for something and then in the next breath claim they're providing that same thing to you at "no charge," but that's exactly what Berkeley is doing. It should also be noted that like other schools, Berkeley also charges for cap and gown rentals, through its on-campus store, for students taking part in the campus-wide commencement ceremony as well as those participating in departmental graduations, which are smaller affairs where students receive commemorative certificates. In 2014, the cost of Berkeley's "Bachelor Gown Package" was $51. The lesson here is straightforward: even when you don't find publicly stated "graduation fees," rest assured that there are likely hidden graduation costs at most colleges and universities.

There are three other important things to note about graduation fees.

First, when these fees relate to clothing, most college graduation fees cover a cap, gown and tassel *rental*. It's not like you're *buying* that apparel and you'll *own* those items as lasting memories of your academic accomplishment. (Your own photos in that academic regalia will have to suffice if you want memories, unless you want to *pay* the school for pictures; more on that shortly). Schools do, of course, make cap and gown rentals available for purchase. That's yet another money generator for certain campuses. But you really shouldn't bother buying a cap and gown from a college or university. It's a total money waster. When and where are you going to wear that getup again? On Halloween?

Second, even if you can't make the graduation ceremony for whatever reason, and you won't be donning that cap and gown, you often still have to pay a graduation fee. For instance, at Texas Christian University, students graduating "In Absentia" nevertheless still have to pay the school's $55 graduation fee.

Graduation fees are non-refundable. They're also often one of the only fees you can't readily escape. If you don't pay the fees, the college or university simply won't release your diploma.

But if you've been paying attention to my general advice, you know that there's always an exception to the rule, and always a way to cut costs. That's especially true for people willing to do their homework, and those savvy enough to ask for a discount or waiver. In this case, as it turns out, some colleges and universities do indeed offer "Graduation Fee Waivers." This benefit is available to undergraduate and graduate students. It's often afforded to military members and some civil service employees; certain scholarship recipients (such as McNair Scholars), as well as part-time and full-time faculty, and their family members. So if your parent happens to be an academic, or if you meet any of these other criteria, look into whether you can get a graduation fee waiver from your school.

Among those colleges offering such waivers are Eastern Illinois University and Chicago State University. Undoubtedly, there are many more. Do your own research to find out about your institution.

One-time Fees

Colleges love to dream up all kinds of ways to charge you additional "one-time" expenses. Most often, these occur as you're coming in the door, as a freshman, or when you're leaving, as a senior. Some common "one time" fees are matriculation and records fees for freshmen and transfer students and "new student" fees for incoming pupils. The list of possibilities is endless and limited only by the imagination of college bean counters whose jobs call for them to create additional revenue streams.

But just because a fee is listed on your bill doesn't mean you should automatically pay it. Question fees that appear out of nowhere or those for which you derived absolutely no benefit. Request that your school remove any charges that don't apply to you; sometimes a call or in-person objection to a fee is enough to get it deleted if you have a legitimate argument. Other students may successfully use what I call the "grandfather clause" in invoking their rights not to pay certain fees. For instance, assume you attend a school that has promised you a fixed rate of tuition and fees for four years. Then, in your junior year, your school increases fees for incoming freshman, still giving a four-year guarantee for their rate of tuition and fees, but also levying additional charges that prior classes had not incurred. If any of those fees wind up on your bill, politely point out to your school that your fees should be "grandfathered" under the terms of the original deal the school struck with you (and other peers in your class-level). If enough students raise their voices in protest, school officials will likely back down from charging extra "one-time" fees and other surcharges.

Parking Fees

Most college campuses charge you for the privilege of having a car on campus while you're a student. You already know from the previous chapter that owning a car will drive up your costs in many ways. Well, now you should add parking fees to the list of expenses you will incur for using your own set of wheels as an undergraduate or graduate student.

Compared to national averages, parking fees at some schools are dirt cheap. For example, the annual fee to park on campus at Buffalo State University is just $70. That's way below the price that most schools charge. In general, you can expect to shell out about $500 to as much as $1,000 for yearly parking. Most schools charge this as an "overnight parking fee"; separate, reduced fees are usually billed as a "commuter fee."

A parking "permit" fee may or may not be imposed separately — in addition to the overnight parking or commuter charges. I suppose that's why the average college in the United States generates roughly $635 per space and about $4 million to $5 million in total annual parking fee revenues, according to recent studies from the National Parking Association.

In 2014, Loyola Marymount University in Los Angeles implemented a somewhat baffling policy under which it automatically began charging car parking fees of $290 per semester to all students taking seven or more semester hours, regardless of whether a student has a vehicle or not. Students without cars have to "opt out" of this cost and request that it be stricken from their billing statements. However, if students don't opt out in time by submitting an online form, they "will be charged $335 without the option for refund," per the school's website and a letter to students from the school's Department of Parking and Transportation.

Other car-related fees that some schools charge are "vehicle boot fees" and "tow fees" — each usually around $50 to $150 — if you get parking tickets on campus and don't pay them.

Hopefully, by seeing the crazy number of car fees you could be assessed, this makes you realize that having a car in college is often far more trouble and expense than it's worth. As already noted, you can shave car expenses — and avoid all these worrisome fees — by doing without a car on campus and using alternatives like public transportation, carpooling or low-cost commercial ride-sharing services.

Printing Fees

A lot of schools charge students to print out those 30-page papers in black and white ink or those color presentations for art class. The costs can be $1 per page. If your school doesn't include printing as part of your tuition and fees, you can probably get better deals on printing at places like FedEx-Kinkos. You should also "think green" and consider whether you're printing too much. Anytime you can deliver homework, a report or other schoolwork via email — or just send documents to someone electronically — consider doing that rather than printing out those papers. Not only will you help save a few trees, you'll also save a few bucks.

Tuition Differential or Surcharges for Certain Majors

Earlier in *College Secrets*, you've read my assertions, and those from others too, that college is a business. For proof of this claim, you need look no further than the emergence of "differential tuition" over the past decade.

Differential tuition is a pricing structure under which colleges charge some students a regular base rate of tuition but then charge other undergraduates — often those who will earn more money after college — higher rates of tuition.

The way it works is that most liberal arts majors at colleges and universities — those studying English, History, Philosophy and so on — will have their tuition charges set at a rate equal to the published, basic tuition and fees you might see on a school's website. But if you're in a pre-professional or specialty program, you'll get hit with extra tuition charges — or a tuition "differential." These additional fees can run in the thousands of dollars annually.

Tuition differential charges are often imposed on those majoring or taking courses in: Art, Business, Drama, Engineering, Music, Nursing, Science, and Theater.

Why are colleges and universities increasingly pricing tuition in this way? School officials offer two explanations. Some say that it costs more to deliver education in these majors. But even more telling, some schools say they're justified in charging higher prices to, say, STEM majors, since those grads are going to command higher salaries after graduation.

Such sentiment flies in the face of the historic mission of colleges and universities, which was originally to impart knowledge and learning — not to try to capitalize off a graduate's future success. By charging certain college students more than others, those at state and public institutions in particular have changed the notion that publicly funded education is a "public good." Instead, the argument seems to be that since individuals (the students) are going to get good jobs as a result of their education, schools (the institutions) have a right to be compensated for that — or at least propped up financially, via higher tuition. That's a sad commentary about where public education has gone. It's a profit-oriented, corporate-type mentality.

Less than a decade ago, differential tuition at the undergraduate level was still relatively rare. Now, unfortunately, it's become the norm rather than the exception to the rule. According to a study by Glen Nelson, an executive with the Arizona Board of Regents, the surcharges imposed by differential tuition average 11%, but can sometimes hit 30% or more.

Some students sidestep tuition differential charges by simply choosing not to take certain courses or major in certain fields. I wouldn't recommend that as a first-line strategy, but I do understand if cash-strapped non-majors would opt to skip particular classes if they simply could not afford them in a given term. It's a shame that students are forced to make such choices. It doesn't benefit them, and it certainly doesn't benefit our society.

Tuition Inflation

Regardless of whether you're attending a private school or a public university, you'll face higher tuition charges year after year in most cases. That's due to tuition inflation, which has recently been in the 3% to 5% range annually. Those tuition rates pale in comparison to what's happened over the past decade —the annual rate of tuition inflation has been more like 8%.

Tuition creep, in the form of ever-rising annual tuition is a hidden cost for most students in America. You can prevent such charges if you attend a school with fixed-rate pricing. But even then, you'd better make sure you graduate in four years, since most tuition plans that keep your rates stable only last for eight semesters.

Other "Hidden" Expenses

Some college costs fall into the category of hybrid expenses — they're a cross between campus-generated expenses and student generated costs. For example, sure you'd like to study abroad — but only because schools keep telling you about how great it would be for your to learn another language or immerse yourself in global business culture. Or, yes, you'd like to join a sorority or the pep squad, especially because, at every turn, your school is encouraging you to get involved with campus groups and clubs. When you do partake in a school's offering, it's your choice, but often at a school's urging. Thus, I consider many of the following expenses "hybrid" costs — generated by both you (the student) and your institution.

Other costs are simply random, oddball costs. These may or may not impact you, but you should know about them nonetheless. With some forethought and planning you may be able to prevent some of these occurrences, thereby keeping more money in your pocket.

So let's turn now to a slew of hybrid, oddball and miscellaneous college costs — as well as my recommendations on how to eliminate or minimize these expenses.

Hybrid Expenses

The seven categories of hybrid expenses include:

A 5th or 6th year of study
Academic fieldwork or research projects
Fraternities and sororities
Internships
Memorabilia
School sports
Study abroad programs and special trips

Here are some pointers on how to manage each of these costs.

A 5ᵗʰ or 6ᵗʰ Year of Study

Nationwide, only about 39% of freshmen at so-called four-year colleges graduate in four years. Only 59% of these students graduate in six years. But many families appear to be completely unaware of these startling statistics — or at least they seem to believe that they will somehow beat the odds.

When Sallie Mae polled students and parents, 92% of them expected students to finish their schooling in five years, and three quarters of those surveyed believed the degree would be completed in four years.

Clearly there's a big disconnect between family *expectations* about graduation and the *reality* of college graduation rates.

Some people blame students for not graduating on time. After all, it's the student who's doing the coursework, or *not* doing it, right?

Others lay the blame squarely at the feet of colleges and universities that aren't doing enough to provide the academic, financial and social support that students need to finish on time.

Studies show that students don't graduate on time due to numerous factors. Some have family challenges, financial issues or academic problems. Some undergrads simply can't afford the institutions they're attending, so these students wind up working too many hours, slowing down their academic progress. Other students don't have the right academic guidance, so they switch majors well into their academic careers or enroll in courses that don't help them matriculate. Any or all of these things can delay graduation.

Unfortunately, the failure to graduate on time is one big factor that needlessly drives up higher education expenses. In fact, the time it takes to graduate is actually a primary determinant of student debt. Research from Sallie Mae has found that upperclassmen are far more likely to borrow than students in their first few years of school. For instance, 33% of freshmen took out loans in 2013, as did 21% of sophomores and 31% of juniors that year. But nearly half of all seniors (45%) had to borrow for college, and a whopping 60% of 5ᵗʰ year students had student loans.

Whatever the cause of students taking five and six years (or longer) to finish school, finger-pointing won't help the situation. But knowing the risk factors for not graduating on time could help you.

In light of this knowledge, push through school as quickly as possible, knowing that the more intensity you devote to your studies — especially by going full-time — the more rapid your academic progress will be. Think twice about switching your major if you've already earned the majority of the credits you need for graduation in that discipline. Be strategic about transferring if you know you'll be using the "two step" college program, starting off at a community college and then finishing at a four-year institution. And choose wisely upfront when it comes to applying to and selecting a college or university. Look for those with better than average graduation rates. Make a point to see an academic counselor every semester — or at least once a year — to ensure that you're making satisfactory academic progress. And don't be afraid to ask for help if you face any setbacks, such as financial difficulties, or even failing a class.

To improve your odds of graduating on time, take CLEP or AP exams in high school when possible. They will accelerate your studies by giving you advanced placement and/or college credit. Finally, consider colleges with 3-year degree programs, 4-year graduation guarantees, or a joint-degree program offering a combined bachelor and master's degree in 4 years if you know you want to affordably pursue graduate studies.

Unless you can beat the odds and graduate in four years, another year or two of college will increase your total costs by about 25% to 50%. This is a major higher education cost which most students and families never plan for in advance. It's also a higher education expense that few colleges will ever bring to your attention when they're encouraging you to apply.

I consider a school's *four-year* graduation rate as critical information for students and parents to know. But many school officials won't come right out and tell you what their four-year rate is; nor will schools readily disclose this data on their websites or in campus brochures. It's even tougher to pin college representatives down on precise graduation data within specific departments, such as the four-year graduation rate for Engineering majors or English majors. When pressed on this, school officials will typically just point to the college or university's *overall* graduation rate; and even then, they're likely to cite the six-year (or 150%) graduation rate, not the four-year rate. Knowing the six-year graduation rate is a helpful measure, but not nearly as meaningful as the four-year rate — unless, of course, you plan on sticking around a campus for *six* whole years to earn your undergraduate degree!

When schools have ridiculously low graduation rates, it signals (in my humble opinion) a major institutional problem that needs to be addressed.

You can't simply blame subpar graduation rates on students alone without looking at the role of colleges and universities in this whole mess.

Schools with very high graduation rates are strategic and committed to making four-year graduations plan the norm — and not the exception to the rule. I recall visiting the University of Virginia in Charlottesville, VA with my daughter and being very impressed by the school's emphasis on graduating students — all students — on time. Sure enough, as it turns out UVA is the number one public school in the country when measured by graduation rates. In fact, it has one of the highest 4-year graduation rates in the nation: 85% of students complete their studies in the normal four-year time frame, ranking UVA right alongside esteemed private schools like MIT and Columbia University, which also have 85% four-year graduation rates.

These schools do a stellar job of graduating students because they invest the time, resources and energy into making sure students matriculate as scheduled. There is adequate student counseling and advising. There is a proper level of academic and financial support for students. There are not major problems in scheduling or course logjams that prevent students from taking classes they need to graduate. And there are a variety of checks and balances in place to ensure that school, personal or economic factors don't derail students' academic progress.

Absent this commitment, students flounder and they simply don't graduate on time.

Knowing these facts, I suggest that students stay away from schools that don't graduate *at least half* of their students in four years. And that's me being generous. Why would you aspire to finish school in four years and then put your trust in a college or university that has consistently shown that it can't get students out of the door in that four-year time frame? It's wishful thinking on your part to expect that you'll be the student who beats the odds. That's what lots of students think — and the odds still wind up being stacked against them. In fact, it *diminishes* your odds of on-time graduation if you enroll at a school with an abominable four-year graduation rate.

For my own children, I will strongly encourage them to focus primarily (if not exclusively) on those institutions with four-year graduation rates of 60% to 70% and above. This approach obviously takes the vast majority of schools out of consideration. So you may not take as sharp a view on this area as I do — and you certainly don't have to. But I would urge you to take a look at four-year and six-year graduation rates, as compiled by the Chronicle of Higher Education, and to give this issue some serious thought. You don't want to later regret being at an institution where everyone is lax about graduation, and students routinely take five to seven years to earn their so-called "four-year" degrees. Be aware too that when schools report their graduation rates, some chunks of students aren't counted at all, such as transfers, part-time students, and students who take a gap year or a break for any reason, and re-enroll either later or elsewhere. They don't count in the figures that get reported — even if they graduate.

Thankfully, *The Chronicle of Higher Education* has completed a major online project called "College Completion: Who graduates from college, who doesn't, and why it matters." This initiative includes a creative online table that makes it extremely quick and easy to see the four- and six-year graduation rates for 1,250 U.S. colleges and universities. Based on their handiwork, you'll see that there are more than 260 higher educational institutions with graduation rates of 50% or better. About 120 schools meet the 70% four-year graduation threshold.

I won't argue that these 120 to 260 schools are always "better" in terms of quality. Education quality is difficult to assess, and a single measure such as graduation rates could never accurately capture quality. But one thing is certain: these 120 to 260 schools definitely produce better *outcomes* — at least in terms of completion rates — than do their peers. It wouldn't surprise me at all to learn that these positive outcomes may also coincide with other good outcomes, such as student learning, and how readily students can find employment after graduation.

Academic Fieldwork or Research Projects

If you could benefit — intellectually or personally — from doing academic fieldwork or research projects off campus, then you should pursue those opportunities while in college.

But realize that these experiences don't come free. Conducting such research and academic work could costs hundreds or even thousands of dollars. Don't take it upon yourself, no matter how passionate you are about a topic, to self-fund this type of work. There's almost always a grant you can get, a non-profit that might help, or even a foundation that would be willing to fund your project if you submit a research plan.

But perhaps the best way to manage these expenses is to apply for departmental or campus aid in support of your efforts. If you hunt around, you'll find that most schools do offer some financial assistance for these initiatives.

At Washington and Lee University, the school awards Johnson Opportunity Grants to rising juniors and seniors as part of The Johnson Program in Leadership and Integrity. Johnson Opportunity Grants provide stipends that support all Johnson Scholars. The program also gives up to 30 other undergraduates — who are not Johnson Scholars — funding to complete various off-campus research projects and internships during the academic year or the summer. The grants range from a minimum of $1,000 to a maximum of $3,000. Students on financial aid who do summer projects can also request an additional $1,500 to cover lost wages. For students, funding through The Johnson Program serves of purpose of "aiding them in their particular fields of study, while also exposing them to experiences that enhance their leadership abilities and hone their ethical decision-making," the school's website notes.

Fraternities and Sororities

Joining a fraternity or sorority can be a fast way to jump right into the life and culture at a college or university and begin to make friends, as well as make an impact on your local school community. But membership dues to join fraternities and sororities are steep: on the order of $1,000 to as much as $4,000 annually at some campuses. Many frats and sororities also do service-based work in far-flung places. So those excursions can cost you extra fees.

"In the Greek system, when a sorority is going on a charitable trip somewhere, of course students want to go," says Suzanna De Baca, the Ameriprise V.P. "These can be wonderful experiences, but students really need to think through all the fees and expenditures that come along with getting involved."

Don't forget also about any charitable contributions that may be expected of you, as well as another big category of expenses when joining Greek letter organizations: clothing for formals and rush events.

In fact, even if you don't join a frat or a sorority, you may still be required to dress up for various events.

"During my MBA program, we had six formals a year. They were optional, but it was a really big part of the business school experience," says De Baca, who earned her MBA from Harvard.

If you can't afford to buy fancy gowns or high-end dresses for rush and formals, rent that attire from places like Rent the Runway, which offers upscale dresses and special occasion attire for a fraction of what you'd pay to purchase those items. You can also borrow something dressy from a friend, or apply for scholarships that are available from most fraternities and sororities.

Internships

Getting an internship while you're in school is a terrific way to get some valuable work experience, make important contacts, and find out whether you'd truly like to work in a given industry. Virtually all four-year colleges in America trumpet the value of internships and most boast about the internship opportunities they make available to students either through co-op programs, corporate partnerships or other initiatives schools implement to help students land internships.

When I went to college, it was hard enough to try to get a paid internship. Most of us that did secure internships did so for a small stipend. But mainly we were sold on the benefits. These days, I'm reluctant to tell students to take on unpaid internships because those are essentially unpaid work hours — hours that could be used to help pay for higher education. All students don't need money from work, however, so it's possible that some undergrads and graduate students too are primarily interested in internships for their own intrinsic value. It's also worth noting that besides some paid internships, most internship opportunities benefit students with college credit and valuable training.

Despite the benefits, there is a disturbing trend emerging surrounding college internships: increasingly, instead of getting paid for these experiences, students are being asked to *pay* for internships. This is going on in Corporate America and government agencies, with third-party marketing firms that arrange for student internships, and now colleges themselves are also imposing fees for internships on students.

Schools say these internship fees offset, in full or in part, their administrative charges and other expenses tied to connecting students with valuable internship opportunities. But I question whether students should be called upon to cover each and every possible administrative cost that schools claim to have. I also don't think colleges and universities should start charging undergraduate students for the school's role in facilitating internships. If that's the case, does that mean certain colleges see themselves as akin to corporate "matchmakers?" Do schools want to now be compensated for serving as middlemen or "matchmakers" between students and companies, government agencies or other entities offering internships? I certainly hope not.

Whatever the case, school "internship fees" are creeping up in many places for undergrads. For instance, at Drew University, students were being charged $350 for internships in the January 2015 term. Flagler College recently charged a $300 internship fee, and an international internship offered via Virginia Tech had a $400 internship fee, plus a $550 administrative fee and a $200 orientation fee. Education students at the University of Alabama at Birmingham were charged a $75 internship fee, while students at Christian Brothers University were charged a $100 administrative internship fee.

I'd recommend that students pass on school internships packed with administrative fees and other unnecessary surcharges. Enterprising students can use their own ingenuity to find other, cost-free internships. At the very least, push back on some of these fees and find out why schools feel the need to impose such expenses. It will probably be interesting to hear certain schools justify the need for these charges — especially considering that for years most colleges and universities have previously borne these expenses without seeking "offsets" or "reimbursements" from students.

Memorabilia

Is there any better way to show your school spirit than to walk around campus with a school sweatshirt or with your college logo on your back? Apparently, many students don't think so. Enticed and encouraged by the constant marketing at their colleges and universities, lots of undergrads in particular go hog-wild over school memorabilia. And it's not just the clothes. It's everything and anything with the school logo, mascot and colors. A lot of it pure, unadulterated commercial overload. But schools would never in a million years suggest you put the brakes on excess spending in this category.

Nonetheless, the solution to this expense is fairly easy: pull back on all buying all school-related gear and remember to stay out of the student store. A lot of that merchandise is over-priced anyway. For basic school supplies that you really need, like notebooks, pens or backpacks, there's no need to get the ones with your campus mascot if that doubles the price. You can go to discount stores like Walmart and get such school supplies for a fraction of the cost than you'd pay buying that same merchandise from your campus store.

School Sports

Colleges throughout the country like to get students to go to school sporting events, games and other sports-related activities. Attendance at sporting competitions is encouraged since such participation demonstrates school spirit, keeps students connected to a school's culture, and can be a way to support the home team. Those things may all be true. But it's also true that collegiate sports help generate big dollars and big business at many U.S. colleges and universities. One way that happens is through schools pushing season passes, game tickets and other sport-related packages on students. Unless a student plans to go to every single game, these packages aren't usually worth it. So if you're not a die-hard sports fan who is certain to be present at every game, you'll typically save cash by just paying the one-time admissions fee and going to the select sporting events you actually want to attend.

Study Abroad Programs and Special Trips

Study abroad is all the rage among many colleges and universities nationwide. Some school officials feel that they haven't done their jobs if they haven't gotten you to expand your horizons, sample international culture and get exposed to some aspect of the global community. This is so important that many institutions are increasingly setting study-abroad targets, such as trying to get 50% of all their students or even 100% of all students to have at least one study-abroad experience. This is especially true for colleges and universities catering to students in business programs, politics and international affairs.

It's great that so many schools are promoting study abroad experiences. But as with many other hidden fees, college officials *rarely*, if ever, bring up the high costs that can be associated with capitalizing on a study abroad program. Until, that is, you're actually ready to do it.

You might have stars in your eyes as you dream of visiting Paris, Barcelona, Singapore or South Africa. But depending on your college, and where exactly you go for your away-from-campus experience, there can be many, many fees you'll encounter studying abroad.

You might have to get certain immunizations or vaccines. Only one out of four Americans has a passport. So if you don't have one, you'll need to get that too, and maybe a visa as well. Most colleges and universities charge students mandatory Study Abroad Insurance, particularly accident and sickness insurance. If your school's plan is too pricey, consider checking out International Student Insurance, which offers insurance policies ranging from $27 per month to $62 per month.

Then there are the study abroad fees themselves, which range from hundreds of dollars to thousands of dollars.

At the University of Texas at San Antonio, students must pay $50 per semester charges assessed on "all students applying to participate in study abroad and exchange programs." After they apply, those same students must fork over another $100 per semester as a "Study Abroad — Exchange Registration Charge."

Meanwhile, at Northwestern University, students receiving credit for their study abroad participation recently paid a "study abroad enrollment fee" of $2,400 per term (for a semester or quarter). There was an exception, though, for students participating in certain options categorized as "Northwestern or Exchange Programs."

That exception highlights a useful tip about study abroad initiatives. Sometimes, going through an official school programs can reduce extra fees. It's also a smart idea to plan these initiatives well in advance and then solicit funding through your department or special scholarships that may be available. Many times, colleges offer financial assistance and resources to those who want to study abroad — but you do have to seek out those support programs because they can be real money-savers.

For example, at the University of Chicago, the school awards 100 Summer International Travel Grants to help undergrads conduct research abroad or engage in intensive language studies. The university also has several other aid initiatives, such as special scholarships to assist those who want to study in a foreign country. You should be aware, however, that there may be tax considerations when receiving such scholarship money. In some cases, if you receive funds to go study abroad, you have to report that money as taxable income to the IRS.

To manage fees, you can also participate in certain free study abroad programs on your own, especially if you mainly want to learn another language.

The National Security Language Initiative for Youth, or NSLI-Y, is a free study abroad program for high school students sponsored by the U.S. State Department. The goal is to teach students one of seven lesser-known languages: Chinese (Mandarin), Hindi, Arabic, Russian, Korean, Turkish, and Persian (Tajik).

STARTALK is part of the National Security Language Institute program. STARTALK is also a project of the National Foreign Language Center, a research institute of the University of Maryland. If you want to learn Arabic, Chinese, Dari, Hindi, Persian, Portuguese, Russian, Swahili, Turkish or Urdu, it's possible to do so free of charge through STARTALK. This program offers no-cost residential experiences abroad, ranging from two to six weeks.

Miscellaneous Expenses

Thus far, we've covered the main categories of school-generated, hidden fees, as well as hybrid fees that are both school-originated and student-generated.

So let's dig deeper now and look at some other "miscellaneous" charges that colleges and universities frequently levy. There are five primary categories of these fees, including:

Card or key replacement fees
Late payment and penalty fees
Official documents
Returned check fees
Service fees

Here's a review of how each one of these nuisance fees can impact your wallet:

Card or Key Replacement Fees

Losing anything that a school issues will result in pesky fees as well. So keep tabs on your student ID card, put your meal card in the same place all the time to prevent yourself from misplacing it, and try to hang onto your room key or dorm keys as well. If you lose any of these items and have to get them replaced, you'll be charged anywhere from $10 to $50. That's money you could put to much better use.

Late Payment and Penalty Fees

Penalties for late payments are stiff, generally ranging from $50 to $100. And these fees are so widespread, I'll bet most students don't escape from four years of college without being hit with at least one late fee (if not many more).

Students: you need to know that if you're a procrastinator, or the type of person who does stuff not just at the last minute, but *late*, that bad habit is going to cost you big time in school. If you're late doing anything at all in college, expect your school to bill you for it. That includes being late to register for a class, late to drop a class, late to turn in a housing deposit, late paying tuition and fees, late to confirm that you're going to do anything in the future. The list goes on and on. And depending on the issue involve, late fees can be quite exorbitant — not to mention unnecessarily bureaucratic.

Remember the $335 non-refundable charge I mentioned that Loyola Marymount University in California charges if you don't opt out of parking? Well, students can get hit with that hefty charge at *any* time because the school requires students to repeat the "opt out" process *every* semester. Frankly, I don't see the wisdom in this policy — unless, of course, the point is for this new procedure to serve as a "gotcha" in order to extract extra fees from those attending LMU.

If a student tells Loyola Marymount that he or she doesn't even own a car, and won't be parking on campus, why does that same student need to *keep* opting out semester after semester? Instead of repeatedly charging a student for parking each semester unless he or she continually opts out, wouldn't a better way to handle this be for the school to have the student's original opt-out notice on file and then to *keep it in force,* unless notified of something to the contrary? This way, there would be fewer demands on the students to go through the opt-out process again and again, a total of eight times over a four-year education. It would also be less administrative hassle and work for Loyola Marymount staff.

There are other late fees you need to watch out for as well, like late enrollment fees. Michigan State University charges undergraduates a $300 late enrollment fee, plus a $200 charge for *each course* added to a student's academic record after the last day of instruction.

Late fees seem to be at their highest, however, if you're ever tardy sending in tuition when it's due. I sympathize with families and schools in this regard. On the one hand, I know how many students and parents are scrimping and saving and borrowing to pay those tuition bills. On the other hand, I also understand that schools need to be able to rely on timely tuition checks.

However, the late fees levied on those who make tardy tuition payments are particularly steep — some might say downright excessive.

At Franklin & Marshall College, where tuition fees exceed $48,000 annually, the school charges a $500 late payment in any semester that tuition is paid late. The same is true at Washington & Jefferson College. At Cornell University, if you register after the sixth week of class and then pay your tuition, you pay a $500 late fee plus an extra financing charge of 1.25% a month, or 15%, annually on late payers.

It's worth noting that tuition and fees range between roughly $43,000 and $48,000 at all three of these schools. So let's assume for a moment that for some reason your family got behind on tuition and you were actually late paying both your fall and spring bills. You'd pay at least $1,000 in penalty fees alone at each one of these institutions.

By the way, I call all these late penalties "sucker" fees because institutions of higher education can move as slow as molasses with impunity. (Just ask any college grad who has waited for about three months or more to get their degree in the mail). But when schools want *you* to act, they seem to have an attitude that, if you don't move quickly, or at least according to their timetables: "Too bad for you sucker! Now we can charge you whatever fee we want!"

The obvious fixes for this problem — at least on the student end — are for you to be responsive to all registration, payment, and other notices you get. Do everything on time and avoid being late. Ever. I know that's a tall order for some, and schools are pretty much asking for perfection in this regard. But abiding by certain rules is part of the process of navigating the higher education system. Also, keep electronic or paper records of everything a school requires in case anyone ever claims you didn't fulfill some obligation. Your documentation could come in handy if you ever need to get a fee reversed.

It would be nice if schools did their fair share as well, like making penalty fees far more reasonable, giving students plenty of advance notice, and telling them about important deadlines and fees in ways other than online messages. I realize, of course, that schools must communicate with many thousands of students at once, so online communication is often the speediest and most cost-effective. Nevertheless since schools are so adept at communicating cheaply and quickly with students via email, how come they can't lower the costs of other digital and email-based services they provide? Does it really cost a college or university the $25 that some charge you for them to basically just enter a few keystrokes in a computer and push a button to deliver an electronic transcript to a prospective employer, an outside scholarship provider or some other third party? I don't think so.

Official Documents

Speaking of documents like transcripts, don't think for a moment that once you've satisfied your course requirements you'll get any academic records free of charge.

Let's say you need a transcript for your auto insurance company in order to get a "good student" discount. That transcript will usually cost you anywhere from $5 to $25. Asking for "Rush Service" will typically push your costs to $50 or so. Even getting your diploma, certain certificates and other college records all come at a price. To save money, get electronic records sent when possible, since they're usually cheaper than paper records. Also, plan ahead and put in your requests with plenty of time to spare since those "rush" fees can be budget-killers.

Returned Check Fees

If you don't have the money to pay a bill, you're better off trying to work out some payment arrangements with your school instead of writing a rubber check. If you do bounce a check to your college or university, you'll get hit with a returned check fee that can be as low as $20 or as high as $60. If the cash isn't in your account and you don't want to face another charge — a late fee — you might consider paying a given bill with a credit card. Just be sure to pay off that credit card in full as soon as possible, preferably the same month, to avoid any interest charges.

Service Fees

If you think late fees are nasty, meet their ugly stepsister: service fees.

Apparently, if your wired or wireless internet service is disconnected, San Diego State University will charge you a $150 "Internet Reconnect Fee" to get you back online. That's nothing compared to some other more outlandish fees. Would you believe that if you are a victim of crime on one of the 23 campuses in the California State University system and need to report the incident to campus police, colleges there are authorized to charge you a $10 "Police Report Fee?"

That's one of the more far-out charges I've discovered. Talk about adding insult to injury.

Colleges and universities also charge you service fees anytime you change your mind about something and it causes them to do the slightest bit of work. So let's say you decide to take time off from school, maybe because of work or family obligations, or simply because you need a break.

At the University of Miami, there's a $100 readmission fee if you leave school and then later want to be readmitted. There's also a $100 reinstatement fee charged if you cancel classes after a semester begins. Another "inactive status fee" is levied as well — apparently on certain University of Miami students in limbo — at a cost of $50 per semester.

At other schools, service fees are really just late fees in disguise. Rather than labeling these charges as the late penalties that they are, various colleges will dub them "service fees" and impose such charges whenever you add, drop or enroll in a class beyond a specified date. Such "service fees" can also kick in if you cancel your housing or your school registration for a term.

Sometimes a change of plans can't be anticipated or helped. But to the extent that such foresight is possible, do your best to stick to the deadlines imposed by your school to decide something, or even change your mind without penalty. Acting in a timely manner is often the very best antidote to incurring these numerous nuisance fees.

Oddball and Random Expenses

Certain oddball expenses can pop up during college too. So be on guard against these:

The Roommate Problem: AKA the Renegade Roommate

Try to pick the right roommate and you'll save yourself a world of personal aggravation and possibly money too. Way too many college students hunker down with roommates that are incompatible and they just wind up driving each other crazy. All too often, the bad relationship spills over into money problems. A bad or "renegade" roommate doesn't pay his or her rent, phone bill or her share of the utilities. Maybe he destroys property or steals something. You get the picture. In these cases, an ounce of prevention is worth a pound of cure. When possible, avoid flaky roommates — including high school pals you know are irresponsible — to decrease your chances of having personal and financial issues related to housing. Roomsurf.com is a social networking site that helps students find compatible college roommates. ULoop.com is another online roommate finder service.

The Torn-up Dorm or Dorm Damage Problem

When you're living on school property, colleges and universities become your landlord. And they have the right to demand that you pay up for any dorm damage or extra wear and tear you create in school housing. Ditto for landlords of off-campus apartments, condos or homes. With an on-campus residence, if there's bad damage — like holes in walls, broken fixtures or windows, or paint and other baked-in stains on appliances or other items — you'll get billed for that and have to settle the bill before you can move out or re-register for the next school term.

If you didn't cause the damage (remember the crazy roommate problem I just mentioned?), then you can certainly write a letter to school officials trying to reduce or eliminate your liability and put it where it belongs — elsewhere. One way you might ward off this issue is by drafting a written "property damage agreement" upfront with any and all roommates. In this agreement, you all agree to live by a certain code of conduct and to individually sign for any damage you might create. Whenever something gets damaged or broken, the responsible party signs the form including a brief statement of responsibility. This way, when the end of the term comes, in theory at least, the "guilty" party has already assumed responsibility for any damage he or she may have done. Presenting this signed agreement to campus officials could get you off the hook for dorm damage you didn't cause. It may also work wonders if you're living with roommates in an off-campus apartment or housing complex.

Now you have a sense of the enormity of hidden costs that you might incur while in college. There were 22 categories in all, including the last two oddball expenses. I know it's been an exhaustive list of fees, and surely some of them you had no clue about before reading this book. At this point, I assure you that you're far better informed about college costs than the vast majority of people out there. In educating yourself, you also know what to expect and how to be a wiser college consumer.

I've tried to walk you through the certain economic realities to give you a firm grasp of the true costs of higher education. If we want to be honest and smart about managing college expenses, then the prudent way to start is to lay everything out and know everything involved — including *pre-college expenses* (as outlined in *College Secrets for Teens*); the *upfront costs* of college, like tuition, fees, room and board; and the many *hidden costs* of college as outlined in this chapter.

Armed with this knowledge, we're ready to move on to financial aid strategies that will get you through your four years of an undergraduate education or even graduate school should you choose to earn an advanced degree. We're in the home stretch now.

So let's get right to it!

PART III

FINANCIAL AID STRATEGIES

CHAPTER 9

HOW TO GET THE MAXIMUM COLLEGE FINANCIAL AID

No matter which higher education institution you choose to attend, you'll do better if you plan ahead — and ask the right questions — in order to get the maximum college financial aid.

"The first question to ask a school is: 'What kind of financial aid do you offer?'" says Pamela Mason, the Senior Associate Director, Office of Financial Aid & Educational Financing, at Columbia University. Brown made her comments at a breakout session called "Financing Your Education" held for students and parents during a recent fall Open House on Columbia's campus.

There are two types of financial aid students can get for higher education from colleges and universities: need-based aid and merit aid.

Unless you come from a very, very rich family that can easily afford to write a check to cover the full cost of college for four or more years, you will require some kind of need-based aid to help pay for school.

Need based aid is tied to your family's economic circumstances, and it takes into account factors such as income, savings and personal assets.

Merit-based aid is completely different. You can be ultra rich or dirt poor and still qualify for merit-based aid, since it is awarded based on personal accomplishments, top test scores, a stellar GPA, special athletic ability or other talents and unique skills.

"Columbia offers need-based aid only," Mason says, adding: "all schools in the Ivy League only offer need-based financial aid."

In addition to the eight Ivy League institutions in America, a few dozen other top colleges and universities — including Amherst, Barnard,

Colgate, Georgetown, Holy Cross, MIT, Stanford, Tufts, Vassar, Wellesley and Williams — also do not offer merit aid. This is very important for families of all income levels to understand, especially if you haven't saved a lot for college or if your family doesn't have a lot of disposable income and you were counting on college scholarships to help pay for school.

The good news about elite schools that don't offer merit aid is that they typically provide very good need-based aid to families, including those earning between $100,000 and $250,000. Some of these schools even have "no loan" or "limited loan" pledges, meaning that their student loan packages will not have any loans — or loans will sometimes be capped at very low, reasonable levels. For these reasons, high-achieving students from low-income and middle-class families should not make the mistake of automatically striking certain schools off their college list just because a school doesn't offer merit scholarships. Likewise, excellent students from more affluent families should also still consider private and public schools that don't offer merit aid, as long as those institutions provide strong need aid.

But if finances are an issue in paying for college, make sure that you have several institutions that offer merit aid on your list of target schools. It may even be wise to focus *mostly* on schools with merit aid, if those institutions are also a good fit academically and personally.

Here are some of the country's top colleges and universities that do offer merit aid: American University, Brandeis, Bucknell, Carleton, Carnegie Mellon, Clark University, Davidson, Denison, Duke, Elon, Emerson, Emory, Fordham, Gettysburg, Grinnell, Harvey Mudd, Muhlenberg, New York University, Rice, St. Olaf, Scripps, Swarthmore, University of Chicago, University of North Carolina at Chapel Hill, University of Southern California, University of Virginia, University of Texas at Austin, and Vanderbilt.

Obviously, this list is not all-inclusive. You'll have to do your own research to find out whether a school offers merit aid, in addition to need-based aid. To get started, check out MeritAid.com; it maintains a list of colleges offering merit scholarships.

Also, realize that simply knowing that a school offers merit aid isn't enough. You should also inquire about what percentage of students actually receive merit aid in order to get a better handle on your chances of nabbing these institutional dollars. With just a little bit of homework, you'll discover that the level of merit aid awarded — and how it's granted — can be all over the place.

For example, at Boston College and John Hopkins University, only about 1% of incoming freshmen receive merit scholarships. Wake Forest says it gives merit aid to less than 3% of incoming students. Meanwhile, the University of Chicago reportedly doles out merit aid to 16% of freshmen, but the school does not award any merit aid to upperclassmen. The University of Miami grants merit aid to nearly 25% of incoming students. For its part, the University of Southern California offers a wide variety of merit aid. The school recently gave merit aid to nearly 30% of first-year students, including full tuition scholarships to more than 100 first-year students and half-tuition awards to more than 200 incoming freshmen.

The Importance of the FAFSA

Regardless of the type of funding your family seeks, the first step you should take to qualify for financial aid is to fill out a form known as the FAFSA, the Free Application for Federal Student Aid.

The FAFSA is an all-important document that determines something called your EFC or "Expected Family Contribution." Your federal EFC is calculated by the government and is a measure of your family's financial strength. Your EFC represents the *minimum* amount of money you're supposed to contribute to your education. (Or if you're a parent, your child's education.)

But be forewarned: no matter what your EFC is, your actual out-of-pocket costs can vary greatly from one school to the next. That's because not all U.S. schools use the FAFSA as the sole way to determine your financial aid package.

About 250 American colleges and universities, mostly private schools, also use another form called the CSS/Financial Aid Profile, which is a separate financial aid application created by the College Scholarship Service of the College Board. (Another 150 or so private scholarship providers also require a CSS Profile when you seek scholarship funds).

When a college or university only requires the FAFSA, it's using the "Federal Methodology," which is a standardized formula that determines your Expected Family Contribution and your eligibility for *federal aid*, such as Federal Pell Grants, Federal Work-Study or Federal Direct Loans.

When a postsecondary school requires the FAFSA and the CSS/Financial Aid Profile, it's using the "Institutional Methodology," which is a different financial aid formula that a college uses in order to award its own *institutional aid.*

So the next thing you need to understand is that your financial aid offer can vary greatly, depending on whether a school is using the *Federal* Methodology or the *Institutional* Methodology.

Adding to the complexity of financial aid is the fact that schools using the Institutional Methodology can tweak the financial aid formulas in any way they want. For example, some colleges will count all your home equity as an asset; while others will cap the amount of home equity in their calculations.

"I have federal rules and I have Columbia rules," says Pamela Mason. "But I do want to get you every single dollar that I can."

Furthermore, a group of about two-dozen elite colleges and universities, called the 568 Presidents Group, use the Institutional Methodology as their base financial aid system. Then they apply another shared set of calculations to evaluate a family's ability to pay for college. This third formula is known as the *Consensus* Methodology.

Pretty complicated, isn't it?

Despite all the nuances of the financial aid system, a basic rule of thumb to know is simply this: in order to get the most possible financial aid, you want your Expected Family Contribution (EFC) to be as low as possible.

A lot of factors go into calculating your EFC. That's why whole books have been written on the FAFSA. One excellent book that I highly recommend is called *Filing the FAFSA*, by Mark Kantrowitz, Publisher of Edvisors.com, and David Levy. (The book is available as a free download on a computer, tablet or e-reader to students and parents who register for free on Edvisors.com at http://edv.cm/ftf14.)

But in the meantime, there are some pointers you should know in order to squeeze the most possible dollars out of the college or university of your choice.

To help maximize your financial aid, here are 15 common mistakes to avoid. All of these blunders will reduce your college financial aid.

Mistake #1: Failing to Do Any Financial Aid Forecasting

If you haven't enrolled in college yet, or even if you are a returning student, there are a number of online tools and services you can use to help you forecast your financial aid eligibility.

You should take advantage of these to at least get a ballpark idea about what your likely college costs will be.

One such tool is the FAFSA4caster, which will give you an estimate for your federal financial aid eligibility.

With the FAFSA4caster, you provide some basic information and the government estimates your eligibility for federal student aid. Using the FAFSA4caster takes less than 10 minutes and you'll need to know just a couple of important data points to get an estimate. One key number you'll have to input is your family's adjusted gross income, or AGI. You can find it on line 32 of your most recent federal income tax return. You'll also need to know the rough total cost of attendance at the school (or schools) you're considering. If you don't already know it, just go to the website of the institution of your choice and find this data; it will likely be in the financial aid section.

In just a few short minutes, the FAFSA4caster will show you what federal grants you might qualify for, such as a Pell Grant. These are typically offered to low-income students. The FAFSA4caster will also show you the federal loans you are eligible to receive. Regardless of income, anyone can get a Direct Stafford Loan in the amount of $5,500. The FAFSA4caster will also let you know if you qualify for Federal Work-Study, which is a federally sponsored part-time employment program where you work either on campus or off campus and earn at least the federal minimum wage, or sometimes more. The national average for work-study awards is about $1,500, but not every college and university participates in the work-study program.

Separately, the College Board also offers an EFC Calculator, to let you predict your Expected Family Contribution for a given school year. This calculator can compute your EFC using the Federal Methodology and also your EFC under the Institutional Methodology for almost any college you input.

All colleges and universities getting government aid — and that's the vast majority of them — are required by federal law to also have

"Net Price Calculators" on their websites. This is another tool you should use in order to help forecast your rough Expected Family Contribution. Your "net price" equals the total annual cost of attendance at a college minus any scholarships and grants you receive. In other words, your "net price" is what you'll pay for a year of college after subtracting free money you get to help lower college expenses.

If you're trying to find a net price calculator on a school's website, search for the phrase "net price calculator" or terms like "college costs estimator" or "financial aid estimator," since some institutions use different names to describe their calculators.

But tread carefully here once you find a calculator. Some schools have net price calculators that are quite good, and others are pretty rotten. Some calculators just spit out estimates that aren't remotely realistic — especially those calculators that don't take into account factors such as a family's assets, how much institutional aid the school typically offers, or the student's academic standing. Without knowing your academic profile, for example, a calculator won't be able to tell you about merit aid for which you might qualify. Another limitation of net price calculators is that they don't let you easily make comparisons across multiple schools.

That's where other nifty tools can help. One excellent tool can be found at CollegeAbacus.com. You start by inputting three top choice schools and then the site asks you a series of questions, mainly financial queries about the student and his or her parents. It takes about 20 minutes total, but it's well worth the effort. After you input the required data, College Abacus tells you your estimated net price at the three institutions you've selected. It also displays the information in a graphically interesting way, making it easy to see and compare everything from the sticker prices at your chosen schools, your anticipated out-of-pocket costs there, as well as the schools' graduation rates, SAT or ACT scores, and more.

College Abacus is a free service that anyone can use, but it's best to try it out before a student's senior year of high school. This way you have more insights into a school's typical financial aid package before you even apply. But remember, all calculators are just estimates; you never really know the exact award a school will offer until you actually apply.

Still, College Abacus is unique in that it uses the very same net price calculators developed by the colleges themselves — calculators taken right from college websites. Then College Abacus marries that info with other financial aid data and formulas, to let you compare your projected financial aid packages across different schools. The College Abacus system provides net price estimates for more than 4,000 post-secondary institutions in the U.S. It's a very robust platform — so good, in fact, that some schools have blocked their data from appearing on the site.

Another nice online tool you can try is the universal net price calculator from the CostOfLearning.com website. This site helps families cut to the chase and get net price estimates for various colleges and universities based on a single data point: your Expected Family Contribution. You simply enter a school name and almost instantly, you'll see a chart showing a range for an Expected Family Contribution going from $0 all the way up to $35,000. So by just moving your mouse to the EFC that is closest to yours, you'll immediately see what your likely net cost will be at a given institution. The site lets you keep adding colleges too, so the chart will plot net estimates for multiple schools and you can see how they compare financially.

The Cost of Learning online tool is free, easy to use, intuitive, and doesn't require you to disclose any personal or financial data.

The federal government has tools too, including the College Navigator site, which provides a range of information on each institution, including costs. There's also a federal financial aid "shopping sheet," that lets families make apples-to-apples comparisons among colleges, just by using consistent definitions.

A final option to consider, if you want a forecast of your likely financial aid, is a paid resource from StudentAid.com. This site creates a customized "College Cost and Planning Report." The basic service is $49 and a premium offering sells for $99. In a nutshell, StudentAid.com gives students an in-depth individualized report, based on a student's interests and colleges of choice. The report, which is done in color and includes easy-to-read graphics and charts, assesses a student's eligibility for aid, evaluates a student's out-of-pocket costs at thousands of schools, and provides detailed comparison data and info on each institution you select.

Despite the abundance of tools and options that exist to help families get an estimate of future college costs, most families don't even know about these tools. So the first time they have any real clue about what their net price, or out-of-pocket costs, will be when they receive an actual financial aid award letter from a school. In my opinion, that's way too late.

Mistake #2: Failing to File the FAFSA or CSS Profile at All

Financial aid starts and ends with that FAFSA form that I've already mentioned. Even if you want to get certain scholarships or merit-based aid, some schools and scholarship providers require a FAFSA, and sometimes a CSS Profile too. (Remember, the CSS Profile is needed to obtain *non-federal*, institutional aid).

Unfortunately, far too many families skip out on filling out the FAFSA — and they lose out on college aid because of this mistake.

According to Kantrowitz's research in *Filing the FAFSA*, 98% of FAFSA filers, roughly 20 million students, submit the FAFSA online each year at http://www.fafsa.ed.gov. Still, about two million students per year — including college-goers from low-income and well-off families — miss out on financial aid simply because they didn't fill out the FAFSA.

Some parents complain that the FAFSA is too long, complicated or overly intrusive. Meanwhile, about half of non-filers who are eligible for money erroneously think they won't qualify for financial aid, so they simply neglect the FAFSA.

This is especially true among higher income households.

Beatrice Schultz, the CFP and college financing expert says: "Nearly 100% of my clients who make over $150,000 assume that they will not qualify for need-based financial aid, and that simply isn't true."

In fact, according to Kalman Chany, author of *Paying for College Without Going Broke*, you should never rule out applying for aid simply because you *think* you or your family might earn too much. "People are often amazed at how much money you have to make in order NOT to qualify for aid," Chany writes in his book.

"Don't assume that because your friend didn't qualify for aid that you won't either," he adds. "There are so many variables it is impossible to say the [income or asset] cutoff is precisely *X* dollars. It just doesn't work that way."

For families with high incomes or relatively large assets, you should still fill out the FAFSA in order to keep your financial options open. You may initially plan to fund college expenses directly. However, you may later wish to borrow money via the federal government, and preserve your cash for investments or other purposes. Only by filling out the FAFSA can you access unsubsidized or subsidized Stafford loans, which may have lower interest rates than other borrowing options.

It's also best to fill out a FAFSA as soon as possible after January 1, since most financial aid is awarded on a first-come, first-served basis. Additionally, many schools and states have financial aid deadlines that occur in the first three months of the year. So even though the FAFSA asks about your income from the previous year, don't wait until late March or April when you've done your taxes. Fill out the FAFSA as soon as possible, preferably in January, using estimates for your prior year's income. You can always go back later and update the numbers once your 1040 tax forms are completed.

For high school seniors starting college in the 2014-2015 school year, and college students continuing their studies in that term, you'll need to fill out a 2014-2015 FAFSA, which was available beginning January 1, 2014. You have until June 30, 2015 in order to be considered for aid in the 2014-2015 academic term, since the FAFSA has an 18-month cycle.

For students attending school the following year, in 2015-2016, you should fill out a 2015-2016 FAFSA, which will be available on January 1, 2015. The deadline to fill out a FAFSA for the 2015-2016 academic year is technically June 30, 2016. But remember: if you're starting school in the fall of 2015 (or any subsequent year), you really should fill out a FAFSA *in the January month prior to* your fall enrollment.

FAFSA forms are also color-coded to help you identify the right one to complete. The section of the FAFSA for *parents'* information is always purple. However, the color for the *student* section of the FAFSA rotates every year among four possible colors. Here's what the FAFSA colors will be for the next several years.

2014 — 2015 FAFSA:	Dark Blue
2015 — 2016 FAFSA:	Yellow
2016 — 2017 FAFSA:	Orange
2017 — 2018 FAFSA:	Green

Before a FAFSA can be completed online, both the student and one of the custodial parents must obtain a Federal Student Aid PIN (or Personal Identification Number). This PIN will be your electronic signature for documents on file with the U.S. Department of Education, including your FAFSA. You get your PIN at http://www.pin.ed.gov.

It's also helpful — but not mandatory — to use a resource called the FAFSA on the Web Worksheet. This document is for your own personal use; you don't have to mail it anywhere or submit it online. Instead, it provides a preview of the questions you may be asked when you do get online to submit the FAFSA. The worksheet also lists the federal deadline for aid, as well as state-specific deadlines for financial aid.

Upon completing the actual FAFSA, if you supply your email to the Department of Education, you'll receive something called a Student Aid Report (SAR) within three to five days. That SAR will summarize your information and will tell you your EFC.

After you enroll in college, you must continue submitting a FAFSA annually to receive financial aid for each school year.

It takes about an hour to complete the FAFSA. But with some effort and a bit of patience, you can definitely get through the FAFSA on your own.

If you really need help, there are many free resources to help you better understand the FAFSA, including the online tips and worksheets offered by the U.S. Department of Education and the National Association of Student Financial Aid Administrators. CollegeGoalSundayUSA.org, a state-based volunteer program, is another free source of help completing the FAFSA. Volunteers are financial aid professionals from colleges and universities along with other higher education experts.

For those with the money to pay, Student Financial Aid Services Inc., which runs FAFSA.com (not a government site), offers fee-based expertise and help. For $79.99 to $99.99, they'll double-check your work, or even fill out the FAFSA form for you.

Although the FAFSA is a free form that costs nothing to submit to colleges on your own, the CSS Profile is not free; it costs $25 to send to one college and $16 for each additional college. Low-income students automatically qualify for a fee waiver when they complete the CSS Profile online, provided they have family income of around $40,000 or less annually, $30,000 or less in assets (excluding a primary residence), and $100,000 or less in home equity.

If you are not sure if your college or university requires a CSS Profile, go to their website or call the school to find out. You can also check with the College Board, which recently published a 2014-2015 list of colleges that require the CSS Profile.

Since the CSS Profile asks more detailed questions than the FAFSA, it usually takes one to two hours to complete this form. So give yourself plenty of time and don't rush the process or wait until the last minute to submit it.

Thankfully, some savvy parents say it does get a bit easier — at least in one way — to submit the FAFSA and CSS Profile in each successive year that a student is in college. The part that gets less cumbersome is that you don't have to re-enter everything each time from scratch. Your past year's information can be pre-populated into these financial aid forms, saving you some time and effort.

Mistake #3: Missing a Deadline

When applying for financial aid, you need to be aware of three deadlines: school deadlines, state deadlines, and federal deadlines.

"Missing a financial aid deadline is worse than missing a mortgage payment. Your bank will probably give you another chance; the colleges probably will not," says Kalman Chany, who is also the Founder and President of Campus Consultants Inc., a Manhattan-based company that assists families with maximizing a student's financial aid eligibility.

Realize that the deadline for financial aid often precedes the college application deadline; at best it might be simultaneous. So always check with a school to know what its specific deadlines are — especially priority deadlines for financial aid and scholarships.

If the college you'll be attending requires your completed application even earlier than the federal or state deadlines, use the school's deadline as the date to submit all your paperwork. That way, you won't miss any deadlines.

About 70% of all student aid deadlines for states and colleges occur *before* April 15; Tennessee and Connecticut have the earliest: February 15.

Perhaps that's why, to get a state grant in Tennessee, education officials suggest applying "as soon as possible after January 1" because awards are made only "until funds are depleted."

In addition to completing the FAFSA form right after it is available, you should be prepared to submit a CSS Profile, if your school requires it, even earlier.

The CSS Profile is available beginning each October. So the CSS Profile for the 2014-15 school year became available in October 2013. For the 2015-2016 academic year, the CSS Profile will be available starting in October 2014.

Again, institutions that require a CSS Profile often have early "priority" deadlines for need-based aid or institutional funds (merit aid). This is particularly true if you are applying "Early Decision" or "Early Action." So for the best chance at financial aid, make sure you know these deadlines and then plan on completing your CSS Profile in late fall — which is *even earlier* than when you'll submit your FAFSA. You will have to estimate income, and that's fine. Just like with the FAFSA, you can — and are expected to — later go back and update your CSS information after filing your taxes.

Mistake #4: Putting Assets in the Student's Name, Not the Parent's Name

If you're a parent, over the years you may have opened savings accounts for your child, or perhaps your kid has nice grandparents who have passed along assets.

It's obviously a good thing to build college savings. But when it comes to financial aid eligibility, having assets in your offspring's name is a no-no.

Here's why: when the Department of Education reviews your income, asset and family information, it will come up with that EFC I've mentioned, or your Expected Family Contribution. The EFC is an indicator of your family's financial strength and colleges use that as a starting point for determining your financial aid package.

To boost your aid eligibility, you want your EFC to be as small as possible. And here's where you may face a problem if you have too many assets in a student's name.

Under current financial aid formulas, your EFC is higher when there are assets in the child's name. That's because all assets belonging to the student are assessed at a 20% rate under the federal methodology (i.e. for schools that require just the FAFSA). Student assets are assessed at a rate of 25% under the institutional methodology (for schools that require the CSS Profile).

By contrast, a parent's assets are assessed at a maximum rate of 5.64% under the FAFSA calculations, and schools that require the CSS Profile assess parent assets at between 3% and 5%.

As a result, for every $10,000 in a student's name, your federal Expected Family Contribution goes up by 20% or $2,000. But for every $10,000 in a parent's name — including accounts like 529 college savings plans — your federal EFC increases by a maximum of just 5.64%, or $564. Under the institutional methodology, every $10,000 in parental assets increases your EFC by a maximum of only $500.

So by strategically positioning your family funds, and keeping large assets out of the student's name, you can lower your Expected Family Contribution and become eligible for thousands of dollars in additional college financial aid.

Mistake #5: Overstating Assets and Income

Another blunder people make in trying to qualify for financial aid is failing to exclude, or omit, certain assets and income as legally permitted.

When you're filling out the FAFSA, pay close attention to every question that asks about your assets and income. This is crucial, as you are legally allowed to leave out certain income sources and various assets you may own.

For instance, when applying for college financial aid, you need not report any of the following as assets: your primary residence, the car in your driveway, a boat you may own or any furniture in your home or apartment. Likewise, do not report untaxed Social Security as income.

If you report these items you will inflate your expected family contribution and lower the amount of aid for which you are eligible.

Making any number of mistakes on the FAFSA will unwittingly increase your Expected Family Contribution, thereby slashing your college financial aid.

"There's a major difference between applying for aid and applying for aid so that you get the most money," says college aid expert Kalman Chany.

"The better educated parents tend to overestimate how well they understand everything going on," Chany says. "But then, their mistakes — due to lack of experience in filling out forms or because they've misinterpreted instructions — wind up costing them money."

At a private college, serious financial aid blunders can cost a family $20,000 to $40,000 over a four-year education, he says.

As a result, "it's sort of penny wise and dollar foolish to try to figure this out on your own," Chany argues. "It's also foolish to try to rely on colleges to help you to maximize your eligibility for money."

With schools using the FAFSA, depending on your income, a minimum of 22% and a maximum of 47% of parents' adjusted gross income may be required toward your Expected Family Contribution.

Among schools using the CSS Profile, a minimum of 22% and a maximum of 46% of parents' adjusted gross income may be assessed toward your EFC.

With both Federal Methodology (FAFSA) and the Institutional Methodology (Profile), keep in mind that the asset and income assessments previously mentioned only come into play *after* a set amount of assets and income have been "protected" by the financial aid formulas.

For instance, the FAFSA grants families a certain "asset protection allowance," which depends on the number of parents in the household and the age of the older parent. This "allowance" means that when the government computes your Expected Family Contribution, it will exclude a certain amount of assets — and not count them in the EFC calculation.

Two parent-households get to exclude a much bigger portion of their assets than single-parent households. For instance, among households with a first-year student in college, the average age of the parent is 48 years old. Under the FAFSA formula, if a 48-year-old is the older parent in a two-parent household, that couple can exclude $33,000 in assets from the FAFSA formula. When there is only one parent in the household, however, even if that individual is also 48 years old, that single parent can only exclude $7,600 in assets from the FAFSA calculation.

A similar process is in place to "protect" a certain amount of income.

For example, depending on how many people are in a household, and how many children are in college, the FAFSA formula shields anywhere from $17,440 worth of income (for a single parent with one kid in college) to as much as $37,020 of the family's income (for a couple with four children and one kid in college).

For a family of four with one child in college in 2014-2015, the first $26,830 in income is excluded from the calculations due to the FAFSA's "income protection allowance." This is the case for both single-parent households and two-parent homes. Similarly, for a family of four with two children attending college, the first $23,840 in income is excluded. Again, this holds true for households with one or two parents.

For all these scenarios, the main point to understand is simply this: only assets and income that *exceed* certain specified amounts are assessed and computed in your Expected Family Contribution.

Here's another crucial tip regarding income: If a dependent student's parents had earned income and adjusted gross income (AGI) *less than* $50,000, the student qualifies for the Simplified Needs Test, a special FAFSA formula in which financial aid administrators completely ignore the assets of the parents and the student in calculating the Expected Family Contribution.

So a family could literally have a million dollars sitting in a bank account, but if its income was $49,999 or lower, those assets wouldn't have to be tapped in order to pay for college. Even better: if the parents' AGI is $24,000 or less, a "Zero EFC" is automatically granted in the 2014-2015 school year. With both scenarios, a student receives more aid.

Mistake #6: Not Checking the Box for "Dislocated Worker" When Appropriate

Unemployment is still high in many parts of the country, and many adults are struggling to find work or secure full-time employment.

If you, a spouse or a family member such as a parent has been downsized, you may be eligible to answer "yes" to the "dislocated worker" questions on the FAFSA. It asks: 'As of today, is either of your parents a dislocated worker?' A separate FAFSA Question also asks: 'As of today, are you (or your spouse) a dislocated worker?'

Being a dislocated worker impacts how your assets are treated and could even reduce your expected family contribution to zero, experts say. So pay close attention to this question and check the box if any number of scenarios is true for you on the day that you submit your FAFSA.

A person can be considered a dislocated worker if any of the four criteria apply:

- He or she is receiving unemployment benefits due to being laid off or losing a job and is unlikely to return to a previous occupation
- He or she has been laid off or received a layoff notice from a job
- He or she was self-employed but is now unemployed due to economic conditions or natural disaster; or
- He or she is a displaced homemaker (i.e. a former stay-at-home mom or dad who is no longer being supported by a spouse, and who is unemployed or underemployed)

Again, even having a parent out of work can make you eligible for additional financial aid.

Mistake #7: Applying Only to Schools That Don't Offer Merit Aid

I've already mentioned the need to have a mix of schools on your search list — including those that offer need-based aid, as well as colleges and universities that offer merit aid. It's unfortunate to learn that a student got in to a very good school, but the family couldn't afford it because they were counting on scholarship or merit aid. If these families had done their homework, they would have known not to count on merit aid from schools that don't even offer such financial assistance.

Mistake #8: Ruling Out "Expensive" Schools Prematurely

A Sallie Mae study, *How America Pays for College 2013,* made some startling findings about how students select colleges based solely on price alone. The study revealed that 40% of students eliminate schools based on price be-fore — even before the student or parent did any research on the college. Another 12% eliminate a college based on price before applying. And an additional 8% will rule out a school based on costs after the student has been accepted but before he or she actually gets a financial aid award letter. Taken altogether, Sallie Mae's data show that 60% of all prospective college students dismiss colleges on because of cost factors alone.

This is a mistake, though, especially if you have great academic creden-tials. You could get merit aid at many institutions. And if your family is low income or even upper middle class, certain "pricey" schools will nonethe-less offer generous need-based aid.

Sooner or later, both poor students (and well-to-do college-bound stu-dents as well), will have to start realizing that a college's published sticker price has little to do with what a family pays out of pocket for a student to attend that particular school.

Mistake #9: Careless Math Blunders

With many thousands of dollars in financial aid at stake, now is not the time to be sloppy or to rush through your paperwork. So double-check everything.

Make sure your last name is listed exactly as it's printed on your Social Security card or your FAFSA will be rejected.

Also, double-check all your numbers and sign your form. Experts say that transposed numbers and forms that lack signatures are two common blun-ders — and both mistakes can slow down or jeopardize your request for aid.

Paying for college can seem like a huge financial burden. But you can reduce your economic stress by maximizing the financial aid you receive and giving the process of filling out the FAFSA the time and attention that it deserves.

Mistake #10: Not Updating Financial Aid Officers When Circumstances Change

If your circumstances or your family's situation changes significantly after you fill out the FAFSA, it's almost always worth notifying the financial aid staff at your selected college.

What kinds of changes are relevant? A couple that is going through a divorce, a parent who loses a job, or an unexpected medical crisis that generates unusually large medical bills all merit reconsideration of your initial financial aid package.

"If there are any changes in your family's finances, let us know," says Pamela Mason, the financial aid specialist from Columbia. A lot of times, the school may ask for more documentation to verify your claims. But don't let that dissuade you from seeking additional aid if necessary.

"When we ask a lot of questions, please don't think it's an attempt to weed you out," says Mason. On the contrary, "maybe your tax return doesn't tell the whole story," she says. "If an external issue affects your family, tell us," she advises, noting that some people may owe back taxes to the IRS, or may be helping a grandparent cover food and nursing home expenses.

"For most parents with more than $250,000 in income, it's rare that they would qualify for a Columbia grant. But it is possible," Mason adds. For example, need-based aid might be granted to families with more than one student in college, to those with special economic circumstances, or even based on the age of the older parent, she says.

But realize the limitations also of trying to go back to schools and get additional aid. While it's true that many schools will have an appeal's process, or will let you fill out a form seeking "special consideration" or a "re-evaluation" based on new circumstances, you should also be aware that sometimes there simply is no additional cash.

By late spring, when many parents start calling to appeal financial aid awards, "most of us don't have any more money," says Whitman Smith, director of financial aid at the University of Mississippi. "So most of us are delivering the message that your package is what it is."

"It's a huge misconception fueled by the media that there's a big pot of money just sitting around unused. That's simply not true," Smith notes. "So we always politely explain: 'We really like your son or daughter, and we hope they can come and that they like what they've seen so far at the University of Mississippi. But if you're looking for more money, the amount shown in the award letter is the full extent of what we can offer.'"

On occasion, if a student improves his or her ACT or SAT score, "we can adjust a scholarship," Smith says, but that's about it.

Mistake #11: Not Understanding "Wild Card" Aspects of Financial Aid

One problem families have when trying to get good financial aid awards is not understanding certain "wild card" areas of financial aid, such as preferential packaging and gapping.

Preferential packaging is when a school offers a specific type of aid package to a student based on how badly the institution wants that applicant.

When a school is highly interested, it will offer the greatest mix of free aid — or it may offer free aid exclusively. This means a college will send an award package that is comprised solely of institutional grants and scholarships. Needless to say, these are the best kind of award letters you could receive.

Preferential packaging is done to meet a college or university's goals. When it's done "in favor" of a given student, it's typically because a school really wants to bring an applicant that offers one of the following factors: alumni relationship; athletic ability, academic merit; ethnicity; gender; geographic diversity; first generation status; low or moderate household representative; and special talents, such as musical or artistic ability.

But there's a flip side to preferential packaging as well. If a school is less interested in luring you to campus, it may grant you admission, but the financial aid package it offers will be far less tempting. For instance, instead of free aid that doesn't have to be repaid, your financial aid package might include hefty loans, or more work-study obligations on the student's part.

According to an NACAC survey, just 15% of public schools say they employ preferential packaging. However, 63% of private schools admit to this practice.

So in your selection process, be aware of your academic standing compared to a college's most recently admitted class of students. If you don't rank in the top 25% or so, you're not likely to receive the most favorable preferential packaging.

In fact, in you're smack dab in the middle, or even in the bottom ranks of a school's academic talent pool, you very well may find yourself getting "gapped."

Gapping occurs when a school offers you admission, but does not meet your full economic need. Under such a scenario, which is also known as "admit-deny", a student is left to his or her own devices to figure out a way to attend that college. In most instances, students are forced to take out massive student loans when they decide to attend schools where they've been "gapped" to a large extent.

Colleges and universities say many different types of students are likely to be gapped, but private schools in particular say students with the strongest academic profiles are the least likely to be gapped.

Unfortunately, students never have a precise window into all of this — and they may not even recognize it when it occurs. In fact, financial aid policies such as tuition discounting, preferential packaging and gapping are increasingly prevalent "because institutions hold all the cards," says Peter Van Buskirk, of BestCollegeFit.com. "They get to define for the family what 'need' is and then they get to define how that need will be met."

There are other "wild card" aspects of financial aid, factors that most families probably never consider.

At Columbia University, where more than half of all students get a Columbia need-based grant, "One of the most important questions on the application is: Where do you live?" says Pamela Mason. "Your zip code matters."

A student's zip code is important because many schools, especially private colleges in the Northeast, make cost-of-living adjustments in their financial aid formulas in recognition that it takes more money to live in expensive parts of the country versus lower-cost regions.

Another "wild card" to be aware of is the very definition of "financial aid." It's not what most families think. In short, "aid" is most often *loans* — not free money. When you receive a financial aid offer from a postsecondary school, that aid package can be any combination of the following: scholarships and grants, which don't have to be repaid, work study, or loans, via the federal government or private loans from the college or university. So don't make the mistake, as many students and parents do, of thinking that "financial aid" means "free money." It doesn't. (See more on this topic in Mistake #13 and Mistake #14).

A final "wild card" in the financial aid world is getting funding when you are an international student. Only about 2% of U.S. colleges and universities — mostly Ivy League schools, elite private schools, the nation's top technology institutes, and flagship public institutions — give any aid at all to international students, according to Kantrowitz. But graduate students who come from other countries to study in the U.S. fare far better. They can often access higher education funding from sources ranging from the Fulbright program to the United Nations.

Mistake #12: Handling Divorced Households the Wrong Way

Lots of students come from divorced homes. So it's also important to know whether a school looks at both parents' incomes, at any step-parents' incomes, or just the custodial parent's income.

Among institutions using the FAFSA exclusively, they take into account the custodial parent's income and a stepparent's income when the parent has remarried.

But you can manage the financial aid process a bit, and get more financial aid, if both parents cooperate in the best financial interests of the child.

"When a student's parents are divorced, only one parent is responsible for completing the FAFSA," writes Kantrowitz, in *Filing the FAFSA*. "The student may qualify for more need-based financial aid if this parent is the one with the lower income."

"To some extent, the parents can control which parent is responsible for completing the FAFSA by controlling where the student lives. This parent, called the custodial parent, is the parent with whom the student lived the most during the 12 months ending on the FAFSA submission date," Kantrowitz notes.

This can be an effective way to boost financial aid at schools requiring the FAFSA alone; again, these are the schools that use the federal methodology. But for schools that use their own institutional methodology, the financial data from both parents will often be required.

Says Columbia's Pamela Mason: "We do expect *both* parents to contribute to their children's education."

Mistake #13: Misunderstanding the Official Definition of Financial Aid or "Need"

You obviously want your financial aid award package to be comprised mostly of free aid, such as grants, scholarships and other institutional funds that don't have to be repaid. Students in the top 10% or even top 25% of a college's student body are more likely to get these funds. So simply striving to be a really good student can help you qualify for institutional/merit aid.

But realize that the government and most colleges and universities consider loans to be "financial aid" as well. Yes, it's borrowed money. And yes, students (or parents) do have to repay student loans. But they're deemed to be "aid" to you nonetheless.

Ditto for "work study" — which is awarded to students who work on campus and get funds to put toward their higher education expenses. Since students have to actually work to earn work-study funds, it's not "free" money with no strings attached; but it's considered "aid" as well.

This need-based aid comes from the federal government; other need-based aid — along with merit aid — comes from the college or university you attend.

To keep your EFC low and maximize a student's ability to qualify for free financial aid, you need to know several things, including how the school determines your "need."

Some schools promise to meet your full economic "need." These campuses want students to be able to afford to come to their schools if the students are admitted. Unfortunately, there's no standard way that all schools calculate a family's need. What you see as "need" and what the schools deem "need" could be two different things.

But some families are surprised to discover that they may have financial "need" even if a student's parents are collectively earning six figures.

For instance, many Ivy League schools, as well as other top institutions with large endowments offer many, many thousands of dollars in aid to families earning about $200,000 or so.

Harvard's policy is that a family at the $180,000 level will pay no more than 10% of its income. Those earning $60,000 or less pay nothing toward

Harvard's published cost of attendance. Families in between those income ranges pay between 1% and 9% of their income annually. Princeton has a "no loan" pledge. It guarantees that it will meet 100% of a family's need with free institutional funds, not student loans. Such a policy greatly reduces student loan burdens for families.

Certain prestigious colleges with big endowments — like Princeton, Yale or Stanford — even give some need-based aid to families with incomes above $200,000.

Clearly, though, most schools don't have the resources to emulate Harvard and Princeton. Besides, these top schools accept fewer than 10% of applicants. But dozens of other colleges and universities promise to meet the full need of accepted students who submit their financial aid applications by certain cutoff dates.

So what happens if you add up all the financial aid you are awarded, your own Expected Family Contribution and any state or federal aid, but you realize there's still not enough money to pay for college? The remaining balance is called your "unmet need."

Think of it this way:

Cost of Attendance (tuition, fees, room and board, plus books and supplies)

minus

Expected Family Contribution = **Demonstrated Need**

Now let's take this formula one step further.

Demonstrated Need

minus

Federal and state aid (like grants or loans); and
Institutional aid (either merit aid or need-based aid) = **Unmet need**

Since everything starts with a school's Cost of Attendance, you first need to know what the college includes or excludes when stating its costs. Some schools lay out multiple categories of costs in declaring their total price tag. These costs are supposed to include tuition, fees, room and board, books and supplies, travel, personal expenses and other miscellaneous costs.

But, as previously mentioned, not every school is fully transparent in outlining costs. Some institutions use small or conservative numbers, or simply omit all categories beyond tuition, fees, room and board.

Once you know a school's total cost of attendance, you can take that figure and subtract your expected family contribution from it to get your total "need."

In other words, if a school's total cost of attendance is $40,000, and your EFC is $10,000, then your "need" would be $30,000. A great financial aid package would cover most of that need with grants or scholarships. If it doesn't, you'll have "unmet need" and will have to consider loans or other financial options.

Mistake #14: Being "Blinded" by Semantics

When selective colleges talk about their admission policies, and the aid they offer, they often describe themselves as being "need blind" "need aware" or "need sensitive."

In theory, need blind schools make admissions decisions with absolutely no regard to a student's ability to pay for college. In other words, just because you might be poor or middle class, and you want to attend an expensive school, a need blind college wouldn't turn you away or reject your application on the assumption that you can't afford the school. If you're qualified, they'll admit you.

A college or university calling itself "need sensitive" or "need aware" is signaling something else. If a college's enrollment is down, or if funding is lacking, need sensitive and need aware schools acknowledge that when making their admissions decisions, they will consider, to a greater or lesser extent, your ability to pay for college.

Despite all the attention this issue often generates, some experts say students and parents shouldn't be "blinded" or fooled by all the talk about whether a school is "need blind" or not.

"You have to put the whole 'need blind' thing out of mind," advises Van Buskirk. "Simply target schools that represent a good fit academically and otherwise."

Van Buskirk laments that there is variability across the board in terms of how colleges and universities will apply various financial aid policies to the same student.

He recalls one student who applied to 19 schools and had a low Expected Family Contribution of just $5,000. The student was accepted at 16 colleges and universities.

"He showed me the financial aid award letters he'd received from the first 10," Van Buskirk says. "They all read his need very differently."

Some schools gave aid right along FAFSA guidelines; others were less generous. "They all exercised preferential packaging, including the only state university in the group that packaged him to just half the cost of the school," Van Buskirk says.

What's more, "a high profile private university gave him aid that initially seemed to meet all of his need," Van Buskirk adds.

Upon closer inspection of the award, however, Van Buskirk had to tell the student that the award letter was actually packaged with loans. "There was a line in there referencing an 'institutional financing option.' That's code for a loan. And that was a $17,000 loan for the first year alone at this school!" Van Buskirk notes.

Such an offer is "total baloney," Van Buskirk says. "When colleges get to make up the terms, it's easy for them to say: 'We meet full need.' And sometimes, the worst offenders are the most selective schools. They lead families to believe that they'll make everything easy for your student to attend."

That's one reason Van Buskirk rails against the notion of any school being totally "need blind." His contention is that unless a school has *limitless* funds — and of course, none of them do — it has to consider finances at some point. That includes a family's finances, as well as the institution's own finances.

"You can't operate as a non-profit in this country without an operating budget. By definition, a non-profit *can't* be need blind," he argues.

Regardless of your take on the merits of need blind schools, be aware that even when schools make a promise to meet full financial need, they're often only bound by that promise if you meet certain deadlines for applying to the school or requesting financial aid. So know these deadlines in advance.

In one NACAC survey, when asked whether they meet 100% of demonstrated need, only 18% of private schools said they did, but 77% said they did not.

Currently, just 61 colleges in the country promise to meet the full need of all undergraduates, according to a survey by U.S. News & World Report, and 46 of those also claim to have need-blind admission. Each one is a private school, with the exception of a single campus, the University of North Carolina, Chapel Hill. (Though it was not included on the survey, the University of Virginia covers full need as well).

There is also a group of need-blind colleges, the 568 Presidents' Group (named after Section 568 of the Improving America's Schools Act), which meets regularly and discusses issues of common concern. As previously mentioned, these schools have their own ways of calculating a family's financial need. But they still leave it up to individual institutions to determine financial aid "packaging" — or the mix of grants, scholarships, work-study or loans a particular school might offer a student.

My advice: take Van Buskirk's recommendation and forget all the labels. Instead, focus on fit, and on getting the answers to financial questions you need to know. Some of the questions you should ask a college or university are:

1. Do you offer merit-based aid?
2. Do you cover full financial need, and if so, how does your school define need and how much free aid is granted versus loans?
3. What percent of freshmen receive grants and scholarships or free aid?
4. How to you treat outside scholarships?
5. Do you provide continuing students the same level of aid as freshman year?
6. Do you have a 4-year graduation rate that's *better than* the national average?
7. Is your 6-year graduation rate *better than* the national average?

8. Does your average freshman retention rate *exceed* the national average?
9. What is the average amount of student loan debt for your college graduates?
10. Do you have a "no loan" or "limited loan" policy, or another specific, clearly defined financial aid initiative to limit college debt?
11. Do you have a job placement percentage that is above the national average?
12. Do you offer free career planning and placement advice to all students?
13. Does your campus offer the opportunity to participate in a regional tuition reduction program?
14. Does this school offer "level" or "guaranteed" tuition rates to students?
15. Is on-campus housing guaranteed to students? If so, for how long?

Getting the answers to these questions will go a long way toward helping you understand how much financial and institutional support a school is likely to offer.

Mistake #15: Failing to Apply for Any Outside Scholarships and Grants

The best kind of financial aid for college is the type that you don't have to repay. That's why scholarships and grants — sometimes called "gift" aid — should be visible on your radar as a way to pay higher education expenses.

When you fill out your FAFSA, you will automatically be considered for federal college grants, such as Pell Grants or Supplemental Educational Opportunity Grants.

Separately, though, you should also seek out other sources of grants and scholarships, through local institutions, community-based groups, non-profits as well as corporate sources. Sites like FastWeb.com are a great place to find outside scholarships and grants that are not offered directly from your school of choice. The following chapter will give you specific advice on winning scholarships.

But by avoiding the 15 mistakes noted in this chapter, and asking the 15 questions just cited above, you can squeeze the most possible money out of federal, state, school-based and other sources of college financial aid.

You'll also get through college with the least amount of economic stress and minimal student loans.

CHAPTER 10

HOW TO WIN SCHOLARSHIPS FOR COLLEGE

Winning scholarships is a dream of many high school teens and college students as well. Who wouldn't want free money for college that doesn't have to be repaid?

So this chapter is devoted to telling you how to go about snagging those scholarship dollars to help reduce your out-of-pocket college costs.

It's important to start with an understanding of potential sources of scholarship funding.

The Truth About Institutional Scholarships from Colleges and Universities

Beyond government grants, the vast majority of scholarship money for college comes from higher education institutions themselves. Scholarship aid from a college or university can come via the school's own money, funds it has received from alumni, donors to that particular institution, or even corporations and non-profits that have established scholarships at a given campus. Regardless of who originally supplies the dollars, when you get these funds, you're essentially tapping into "institutional" college scholarships.

By applying to schools that offer merit aid, and targeting campuses where you rank academically in the top part of a school's student body, you can greatly increase your chances of earning these free institutional scholarships. In many cases, you need not submit a separate application for these scholarships; you are automatically considered for them when you apply. In other instances, however, you will have to apply directly through a college department or a specific university program to put yourself in the running for competitive school-based scholarships. These scholarships are merit-based aid, granted to students in recognition of their academics, athletics, or some other special talent. Some merit-based scholarships also require that you fill out the FAFSA, so it's important to do that, always.

It's also crucial not to make assumptions about whether you will or will not get scholarships. For example, many middle class or well-to-do students mistakenly assume that they won't get scholarships simply because they have higher incomes.

But a Sallie Mae study, called "How America Pays for College," found that students from wealthier families are actually *more* likely to receive larger scholarship awards than students from low-income families. The report revealed that 36% of families with an income of $35,000 or less receive an average of $7,237 a year in scholarships while 35% of families making $100,000 or above receive $10,213 a year.

Furthermore, a recent report from the New America Foundation showed that public and private colleges are shifting their scholarships to mostly merit-based aid — rather than need-based. So don't jump to conclusions about whether you'll qualify for scholarship funds of any kind.

Finding Private Scholarships

In addition to pursuing scholarships directly from a college or university, many students also seek outside scholarships from third-party sources. These are sometimes referred to as "private" scholarships.

When your funds are low and you need additional aid to attend college, it's a good idea to explore all your financial options. Perhaps you want to apply for scholarships because you've heard of students who went all out and earned enough scholarship money to pay for a year's worth of school expenses — or even all four years of their college education. That does happen. But it's rare. According to college expert Mark Kantrowitz, who is also the former publisher of the scholarship site FastWeb.com, only about 7% of students win private scholarship funds for college, and the average award is just $2,500.

Knowing these statistics, you should hunt for outside scholarships in a very strategic way — to get the best possible results, and to avoid wasting time and energy in a fruitless quest for dollars.

To help you land that free money, here are 12 steps to greatly increase your odds of winning private scholarships.

1. Start early
2. Treat it as your job
3. Use technology
4. Go local
5. Tap personal and family ties
6. Get organized
7. Avoid scholarship scams
8. Obey all rules
9. Study past winners
10. Personalize your entry
11. Follow up
12. Wash, rinse, repeat

Let's examine each of these steps and see how you can put this advice into practice, giving yourself a much better chance at winning scholarships for college.

1. Start Early

Starting your scholarship hunt early will help you in multiple ways. For starters, you'll be able to get more organized and approach your search in a more systematic way. You'll also avoid one of the main traps that students fall into: waiting until the last minute and then rushing their scholarship applications and essays. Finally, starting early allows you to submit your application sooner rather than later. Sometimes this is a desirable for scholarships where funds are doled out on a rolling basis. In such instances, the money lasts only so long. It's "first come, first served." So the quicker you get in your scholarship materials, the more likely you are to reap a financial benefit before funding evaporates.

There's another way to look at the advice to "start early" — not waiting until your senior year of high school to seek scholarships or to apply for them.

When my oldest daughter entered high school, I figured we'd get an "early" start by looking for scholarships when she was in the 9th grade. Boy, was I wrong! Little did I know that we were (in some ways) actually a bit late when it comes to nabbing scholarships, grants and free money to help pay for college.

Why would 9th grade be considered late?

Well, did you know that there are educational scholarships for kids as young as five or six years old? That blew me away! But this knowledge also made me even more determined in the hunt for scholarships. After all, in addition to my first-born daughter, I have a teenage son and another younger daughter as well.

Sure, we're saving for our kids' college education with 529 plans. But I'm also realistic enough to know our savings won't be enough to cover the full costs of all three kids' education, considering the ever-rising price tag of a college education.

From a timing standpoint, always remember that there are two primary times you should be in the hunt for private scholarships: in the spring and the fall. Scholarships with spring deadlines often require you to submit your applications in April or May. But many scholarship deadlines occur months before that — in the prior October or November. So for high school seniors, plan on sending your first scholarship applications in during the late fall season of senior year.

2. Treat it as Your Job

Students sometimes hate to hear this advice: but in order to do justice to a scholarship search, you need to think about it as your full-time job. OK, so you may not have to spend a full 40 hours a week on it, but at least act as if it's a *part-time* job. That means taking a good 15 to 20 hours per week to launch into your scholarship hunt.

Those hours will be spent researching scholarships and grants, making sure you meet eligibility requirements, compiling a resume, putting together applications, writing essays, soliciting recommendation letters, and more. You'll likely have to do this for several weeks (even if the time is spaced out over a few months).

Successful scholarship winners — and I won a few scholarships of my own back when I attended graduate school at USC — will tell you that you'll only get out of your scholarship search whatever you put into it.

Treating the scholarship process like a job also entails doing things professionally — not in a half-baked manner. So prepare yourself to fill out all forms to the best of your ability, typing up documents, keeping them clean, and presenting a super polished package of materials whenever something must be sent via mail.

Another thing I've learned: getting scholarships is largely a numbers game. Not only do you have to be "in it to win it," but you also have to be committed to applying to a lot of scholarships. Three or four won't cut it. Plan on applying for at least a dozen — two dozen is even better — to greatly improve your odds of landing one or more scholarships.

Does this mean a lot of time spent on your scholarship search? Yes, absolutely. But the payoff is more than worth it. Getting thousands of dollars worth of scholarships now — for yourself or your child — means you won't have to do things like take out unnecessary student loans, tap home equity, or use credit cards to pay for various college expenses. So if you're really serious about winning scholarships, yes, you do have to make it at least a quasi part-time job.

The final aspect of treating your scholarship search like a job is to think as job hunters do: they first cast a wide net and then they narrow their search. For example, job hunters will often look through the classified ads of the local newspaper or get online at job and career sites like Monster. com. But once they do start searching, they find all kinds of jobs — for retail industries, sales, banking, administrative work and more. Obviously, a strategic job hunter won't apply haphazardly to all of these positions; he or she clearly wouldn't be qualified for all of them. By the same token, you should survey the landscape — as a good job hunter does — and then only apply to those scholarships for which you are very qualified. Otherwise, you're really just spinning your wheels.

3. Use Technology and Social Media

One way to "cast a wide net" and see what's out there in terms of scholarships is to use the Internet. There are a number of websites that allow you to set up a scholarship profile, and then these sites with alert you to, or connect you with, scholarships for which you are a good match. Some good scholarship websites include: CollegeGreenlight.com, Fastweb.com, Scholarships.com and ScholarshipExperts.com.

If you don't set up a scholarship profile, you'll miss out on a huge number of scholarship options. So it's definitely worth the 10 or 15 minutes it takes to create your online scholarship profile. In fact, I recommend setting up accounts at two or three scholarship websites for optimal results.

Technology can aid you getting more scholarships in other ways too: like helping you discover opportunities via social media, making it easier for you to complete multiple scholarship applications without retyping everything again and again.

On the social media front, you can search for various hashtags on Twitter — like #scholarships, #grants or #moneyforcollege and find new sources of free money.

Additionally, some young people use social media platforms as a form of fundraising, from relatives and friends — as well as from complete strangers who simply want to help a student go to college.

Separately, online tools like Scholar Snapp let you re-use your information and apply for more scholarships in a way that's fast, easy and free. Fastweb.com, Scholarships.com and Zinch.com all use the Scholar Snapp solution, which makes it a breeze for you to complete numerous scholarship applications without the hassle of re-entering your personal data every time you apply for new funds.

4. Focus Mainly on Local Scholarships

Because college bills can be so large, some students only want to apply for big national scholarships, such as those offered by Coca Cola, Intel or other major corporations. And then there are college students who only go after prestigious national awards, such as Marshall Scholarships, Rhodes Scholarships, Harry S. Truman Scholarships, or the Barry M. Goldwater Scholarships. All these scholarships can definitely pay big bucks, but the problem is that there are so many students vying for them that you'll face very stiff competition. If you're very academically qualified, and if you're willing to put in the work to apply for these scholarships, then by all means go ahead and put a few of these on your list.

But you'll fare far better overall by focusing on local scholarships that are right in your own backyard. Not only do local scholarships have less competition, they're also typically designed specifically for students just like you. For example, there may be non-profit groups or companies in your particular city, town or county that *only* give money to regional students. These entities often want to support "homegrown" talent. That gives you a remarkable edge when going for these awards as compared to the long odds in national competitions that will attract students from all over the country.

To think locally, consider a host of questions:

Are there city/township, regional or state scholarships for which you might be eligible?

Are there community organizations or local civic groups that offer scholarships?

Are there schools — like your own high school — that provide scholarships for area students?

Are there religious groups or non-profits you could contact to request scholarship info?

5. Tap Personal and Family Ties

Once you go beyond the local angle, you should also think about what personal and family ties you can leverage in order to home in on even more targeted scholarships. For example, you should make a list of any and every membership group or affiliation you and your parents have. For a student, this might include student clubs or community based affiliations you have. For parents, they often have professional memberships, ties to trade groups and industry associations, as well as social or civic connections.

Even if you or your parents are not members, a variety of organizations offer scholarships to regional students. But members will probably fare best when seeking scholarships from service organizations and groups like your local Chamber of Commerce, Kiwanis, Rotary Club, Circle K, Key Club or Jaycees.

Community Foundations are another great local resource where you can seek scholarships. The Community Foundations National Standards Board, a supporting organization of the Council on Foundations, maintains a Community Foundation Locator service showing you community foundations throughout the country.

Don't forget, too, to look into whether your place of employment offers scholarships. Many companies — especially mid-size and large corporations — do offer scholarship plans that benefit the dependents of their employees.

6. Get Organized

Once you begin to research all the scholarships that are out there, it may feel a little overwhelming. That's why it's important to be organized so you help narrow your search to those scholarships that best match your academic or personal interests, as well as your unique profile.

When you have a list of likely scholarships for which you will apply, keep track of them in a systematic way, preferably by compiling an online list of targeted scholarships. Some students (and parents) may prefer to keep print outs and files of scholarships; that's fine too. Just be sure your record-keeping system is accurate, easy to use, and that it works for you.

The key points of information you'll need to record to stay organized are:

- The name of each scholarship and the sponsoring organization
- The contact info for the organization: website, phone number and address
- The deadlines for each scholarship, grant or contest
- Key dates (when you requested, received, sent in or mailed an application)
- Requirements: such as essays, transcripts or letters of recommendation

Beyond these things, it's also a good idea to have multiple copies of your resume or an activities profile about yourself, showing work experience, awards, community involvement or other personal and academic highlights.

7. Avoid Scholarship Scams

Unfortunately there are con artists out there preying on scholarship applicants, waiting to get you to pay them a fee or simply to get your personal information so they can commit identity theft. So be vigilant when you're hunting for scholarships and keep alert to some basic red flags.

You can avoid becoming the victim of a scholarship scam just by following a few simple guidelines. Never believe a so-called scholarship finder or provider if they make any of these claims:

- **You don't have to do any work**: If someone says they'll do all the work for you, know that it's a bogus deal. Don't walk, run in the opposite direction because it's nothing but a scam. A real scholarship provider won't want some third party to fill out your applications and write your essays for you. Doesn't that seem ludicrous? So don't believe such tales if someone offers to "do all the work" — in exchange for a big fee.

- **We have the "only" access to this scholarship**: Again, this is a telltale sign of a con. Why would a legitimate scholarship group grant one company "exclusive" access to get the word out about a scholarship? It doesn't even make sense. Just say "thanks, but no thanks" if you come across an offer like this.

- **This scholarship requires a fee of just $399**: Whoa! Stop the bus! Big red flag here. Anytime someone is charging you a hefty upfront fee, either as an "application" fee or for something else in connection with a scholarship, you should smell a rat. Even if someone says they're fee is for "helping" you with the process, do you really need to pay 400 bucks just for them to fill out an application? No, you don't.

- **This scholarship is 'guaranteed'**: By definition scholarships are competitive, or at least open to multiple applicants. So why should any one person have the inside track to "guarantee" that you'll win a scholarship? Such claims can't be backed up, and you'll only end up falling for a scam. So stay away from scholarship marketers making this tempting (but utterly false) promise.

8. Obey All Rules

This should go without saying, but make sure you follow all scholarship rules and requirements — and I mean *every single one!* It's way too easy to have your application disqualified simply because you failed to adhere to published guidelines. So if a scholarship sets an essay limit of 500 words, don't make yours 501.

If the deadline is Sept. 30th at 11:59 pm, that doesn't mean midnight. In fact, if you follow my earlier advice, you won't be one of those last-minute stragglers. You'll have your scholarship application in *early*, well ahead of the deadline.

It's important to follow other rules, too, including eligibility guidelines, deadlines for submitting letters of recommendation or supplemental materials, and even formatting instructions or online submission criteria, if a scholarship committee expresses preferences about that.

And above all: please don't give a scholarship organization something it clearly does not want. If they specifically ask for *two* letters of recommendation, don't think that *three* will be even better. It won't. It will likely just get your application thrown out for failing to follow rules. Ditto for sending in extraneous materials that weren't asked for or required. That video of you performing community service or singing, or that science project you did, or that interesting art portfolio of yours — keep all that to yourself, unless such "extra" material is specifically requested. In most cases, with scholarships, less is more. So don't make the classic mistake of inundating a scholarship committee with a ton of extraneous stuff it doesn't need in order to evaluate your or to make a decision about you getting a scholarship.

9. Study Past Winners

Another way to boost your chances of winning a scholarship is to research past winners and try to spot trends. By examining prior successful scholarship applicants, you should be able to get a sense of what you'll have to do to be competitive. What do all the winners seem to have in common, if anything?

Were they all academic standouts, or did they all show a great deal of compassion toward others? Did their essays or projects seem offbeat or humorous, or very serious and professional? This information will give you some insights into the "tone" that may appeal best to the scholarship committee.

Consider also how previous scholarship winners related stories about themselves. Did they share experiences from junior high or even middle school, or did they mainly focus on their high school or college experiences? Learn from their success and emulate it where appropriate.

10. Personalize Your Entry

A nice way to help your scholarship bid is by standing out from the pack. So once you've assembled all your materials to mail, or have prepared to submit everything online, spend some time thinking about one or two ways that you can create a "personal touch." Some students opt to send in a photo of themselves in order to help the scholarship committee see the student behind the application. This can be an effective way to help "put a name with a face," so to speak. But again, be careful not to violate any rules of throwing in extra, unsolicited materials. So only include a photo if a) you have a good photo to send; and b) it's clear from the instructions that doing so would not violate any scholarship rules. If in doubt about the latter part, call and ask.

Another way to personalize your scholarship submission is to simply tell the committee something about yourself from the heart. Just like when you complete college essays, your scholarship essay should reveal something about you that can't be seen in your transcripts, grades or test scores. Maybe you've overcome shyness or a stuttering problem and you now tutor local students or your peers at school. Or perhaps you have a fondness for crystal figurines or snowboarding and you can somehow tie either one of those passions (or both) into the scholarship you're seeking. Whatever the case, by sharing something about your own personal life and your own story, you make your application more unique and memorable.

11. Follow Up

This is one of the least utilized steps that students take in the scholarship process. But if you are truly treating the scholarship hunt as a job (remember step 2?) then you should be professional and follow up. This is especially true if you win a scholarship. Then you *really* need to exercise professional courtesy and follow up with a written letter of thanks.

Tell the scholarship committee how you'll use the money. Express gratitude. Be humble but appreciative. Scholarship sponsors love to know that the work they've done will support the work you want to do. It's part of their mission and their reason for existing. So it truly does give them great pleasure to know that their support has made a difference. No matter how small or how large a scholarship you might earn, always, always follow up with a thank you note.

Even if you don't win, you should consider following up with strategic organizations. For example, if it's a small group that didn't have too many applicants, you might send a short note of appreciation, thanking the committee for considering your application, and perhaps even asking for feedback — especially if you plan to apply again for the scholarship (assuming you remain eligible).

That's not practical in a large scholarship contest, where thousands of applications have streamed in. But in a small scholarship, or one that was local and where you might even know a scholarship committee member, you can ask for suggestions on how to improve your application or even tactfully let them know that you appreciate the consideration and that you'll re-apply the following year — again, assuming you still qualify.

12. Wash, Rinse, Repeat

The final step in increasing your chances of earning scholarships is to replicate the process all over again — wash, rinse, repeat — for the rest of the time you're in college. One of the biggest blunders students make in finding and securing scholarships is that they simply give up seeking them after their freshman year in college. Doing that, especially if you've already won an award, is likely leaving free money on the table.

You actually have better odds of winning a scholarship when you're an upperclassman, since most college juniors or seniors won't keep applying for scholarship funds. Plus, some collegiate scholarships can be $10,000 to $20,000 or more, so they're definitely worth pursuing.

As a final word about scholarships, do understand that there is truly something out there for everybody, including young and older students and non-traditional applicants as well.

For example, Youth For Understanding USA offers scholarships for study abroad. Our Next Generation offers scholarships to support attendance at pre-college programs. There's the prestigious Jack Kent Cooke Foundation Undergraduate Transfer Scholarship, the nation's largest private scholarship for community college transfer students. There are even scholarships for undocumented students.

So you'll want to actively seek out scholarships for which you may qualify based on everything from your gender, ethnic, racial or religious background to your chosen major, future career path and current hobbies and extracurricular interests.

Don't think scholarships only go to poor students, minorities, high school kids with "A" grades or the children of alumni. If you are willing to put in the work, I can guarantee you that there are scholarships available that are tailor-made just for you.

Good luck in your scholarship hunt!

CHAPTER 11

How to Borrow Responsibly With Student Loans

For many people trying to earn a college degree, student loans seem like an inevitable part of paying for school.

Since college costs are so high in the United States, most average-income families can't imagine being able to pay for higher education without taking on debt — or without some sort of significant outside support. But any one who wants to get a college education can reduce the need for borrowing, and drastically cut school costs, just by following two steps:

1. Choosing the college or university that is the best "fit" for a student — academically, personally and financially; and
2. Knowing the true cost of college, and planning for everything accordingly

When taken together, what each of these two steps does for you is simple: they help you to *become a much smarter college consumer.*

The first step mentioned above is all about the college selection process. The school you choose to attend will greatly determine your higher education costs. By evaluating a range of campuses that represent the best fit for you, you'll not only increase your chances of admission to a host of colleges and universities, you'll also greatly boost your chances of getting free money from those institutions. If you can snag no-strings-attached money from a college or university, such as scholarships or grants that don't have to be repaid, you'll greatly reduce the need to take out student loans.

In the companion book in this series, *College Secrets for Teens*, I explore the range of *pre-college* expenses that students and families face, very much like I've just outlined for you the *upfront* expenses, as well as the *hidden* costs of college in this book. Remember: knowing about *all three areas*—pre-college bills, upfront costs and hidden expenditures—is vital to having a true understanding of total college costs.

Equally important, though, in *College Secrets for Teens*, I give concrete advice and easy-to-follow tips on how to find the best college fit, using a variety of strategies and simple, straightforward ways to analyze schools. As college expert Peter Van Buskirk notes, when you find a college with the optimal fit, that school values you for what you have to offer, so it *rewards you financially* with either merit aid or with need-based aid.

Have you heard the expression: "Beauty is in the eye of the beholder?" The college admissions process — including obtaining merit aid or need-based aid — is a lot like that. For better or worse, getting in to a good school, and then securing adequate funding from that campus, is a bit of a "beauty pageant." A student that strikes one college as a "perfect fit" — a "beautiful" applicant, if you will — may not strike another college as especially appealing. Remember the story I shared in the introduction to this book about the big difference in my experience with Boston University versus USC? That's an example of this "beauty is in the eye of the beholder" phenomenon in the world of college admissions and college funding. So you have to know how you're viewed by a given institution, what it takes to make yourself more "attractive" to a school, and how to determine which schools value you most.

Selecting the right college or university — one that values you for your academics, special talents, hobbies, diversity, personal interests, or other factors — is directly tied to the *financial incentives* that a school will provide to woo you to its campus. So for those of you who have not yet entered college, I urge you to check out *College Secrets for Teens*. I promise you, it will help you and your family save a ton of money — right now and after you enroll at the college or university of your choice.

By taking the suggestions offered in *College Secrets for Teens*, you'll have the guidance you need to find the "best fit" college, which takes care of step #1 mentioned above.

By making it this far and reading this book, *College Secrets*, you now know the true, total cost of college, which is step #2 recommended above.

So congratulations! Believe it or not: you've already tackled most of the heavy lifting.

But what if you're currently in college, or you're about to enter school and you've determined that there's *no possible way* you can go without loans? What should you do?

This final chapter of *College Secrets* is designed to help you figure out *if* you should borrow money for higher education, and if so, how to go about doing it in the best possible manner.

It obviously helps if you (or most likely, your parents) have started planning for your college education earlier, rather than later. But if you're a late-starter, you needn't despair and think that college is out of reach. Nor should you assume that you'll be shackled with debt forever — not as long as you borrow responsibly for your education.

What is a "responsible" level of student loan debt? There is no exact definition of this concept although there are several guidelines and rules of thumb you can use to keep you in a relatively good "safe zone" when it comes to college loans. I'll share them with you shortly.

What every one agrees on, however, is that it's in your best interest to avoid excessive amounts of student debt.

Student loan debt in America tops $1.2 trillion, and more than 70% of U.S. college grads from the class of 2014 had to borrow for their bachelor's degrees. Among those graduates, their average student loan burden was $33,000, according to Mark Kantrowitz, the college-financing expert who has completed an analysis of recent government data. That makes 2014 degree holders the most indebted class ever — an unfortunate distinction, and one that will probably be topped by future grads in the class of 2015, and then 2016, if current trends continue.

Fortunately, you can definitely borrow responsibly using student loans if you use the following six strategies.

1. Borrow as a last resort, not a first choice
2. Set borrowing limits and stick to them
3. Always get federal loans first
4. Understand all your loan options
5. Pay a little along the way
6. Stay out of default

Let's evaluate each strategy and see how some basic knowledge about student loans can help you finance a college education the proper way.

Borrow as a Last Resort, Not a First Choice

I'm convinced that far too many students and parents facing college bills borrow needlessly for higher education, simply because they make borrowing a *first* choice rather than a *last* resort.

Just because a tuition payment is looming or you need to buy costly school books next semester, and you don't have the cash on hand, that doesn't mean you should automatically resort to borrowing and going into debt to cover those expenses.

Whether you're looking at near-term bills or planning ahead for college costs over the long run, you will always come out better financially if you evaluate all possible resources and options before you consider borrowing.

For some people, this very notion — of borrowing as a *last* resort — requires a shift in mindset. America has become such a debt-ridden, consumer-driven culture that whenever we can't afford to pay for something in cash, our *first* instinct is to think something like: "Oh well, I'll pay with a credit card," or "I can always take out a loan."

That kind of thinking can get you into trouble with your everyday spending and regular monthly obligations. It can also lead to financial ruin when it comes to planning and paying for major expenses, like college bills.

A better strategy, rather than always defaulting to loans and credit, is to first truly assess whether borrowing is necessary at all. In this case, before you take out student loans, you should consider whether you've pursued a range of other options, such as:

- Scholarships and grants
- Paid internships
- Work study or part-time work
- The student's own resources
- Parental or family resources

Here's how each one of these options can help you stay out of excessive student debt.

* * *

Scholarships and Grants

On the scholarships and grants front, please don't tell me that you applied for three or four scholarships and didn't get any. In my opinion, that's not a big enough effort. When money is truly an issue, you have to be willing to put in some serious work in order to get the payoff you need. It's that simple. As you learned in the previous chapter, part of getting outside scholarships and grants is "playing the numbers game." The more scholarships you seek, the better your odds of landing some cash that can help you with college bills — and help you avoid student loans.

Don't waste your time indiscriminately applying for scholarships you don't have a realistic shot a winning. Instead, as suggested earlier, focus your efforts on local scholarship opportunities and those that are well-suited for you based on your unique talents, family history, memberships and affiliations. If you've applied for at least a dozen scholarships — or as many as 20 if you've been aggressive in your scholarship and grant hunt — then you've truly satisfied this criteria and you can move on in the process of considering student loans.

Paid Internships, Work-Study and Work Opportunities

Paid internships and work opportunities while you're in college are other money-generating steps you could take to avoid student loans. Notice that I said "paid" internships, not unpaid ones. When you're trying to scrape up money to pay for college and prevent unnecessary student loans, you just don't have the luxury of taking on internships for which you receive no financial compensation. If your situation changes later, you can adjust accordingly. But for now, if internships are an option, only choose those that offer to pay you for your efforts.

If your college financial aid package includes an offer for you to participate in work-study on campus, you should strongly consider accepting it. The work-study program is a good way to help pay for higher education. Alternatively, you can find part-time work on your own — either on or off campus. It's best if you can work in a job that will give you experience in your major or the field you'd like to enter professionally once you graduate. But if that's not possible, simply find the best-paying, most rewarding job you can to help pay for your school expenses.

I recommend capping internship or work obligations at a maximum of 20 hours per week. If you can limit time spent on an internship or your job responsibilities to a range of 10 to 15 hours per week, that's even better. Again, these are methods to earn money that could be used in lieu of student borrowing.

Student and Parental or Family Resources

If you're ready to borrow for college, you may be considering that option because you think you've fully tapped all available resources you have or that your parents can offer. Maybe that's true. But maybe it isn't.

In looking at your own resources, is there something you can sacrifice that might help out with your college education? For example, if you happen to own an automobile, but now you're having second thoughts about taking it to school, are you in a position to sell your car? The funds raised from that sale could go a long way toward knocking out college bills.

You may also be able to raise money in other ways, through relatives or even friends. By tapping into another resource you have — your family and social network — it's possible to drum up cash for college. Instead of getting a sweater each year from your grandmother, or certain material gifts from your loved ones, why not write an "update letter" letting everyone know about your college ambitions? If you do this prior to the end-of-year holidays, you could tell relatives that in lieu of any store-bought gifts they might offer, you'd be very appreciative if they could instead provide you with cash to help lower your college expenses. Make it a nice, personal letter, of course, not just an appeal for funds! Give relatives an update on your school progress, inform then about your class-based activities and your extra-curricular pursuits, and advise them of your future educational goals, too. It's in that context that you can also tactfully mention your preferred holiday gift: money to help offset your college costs.

Some students may prefer to send an "update letter" in the mail, others may rely on email, and still others will choose social media channels to get the word out. Use whatever form of communication you feel would be best received, considering the individuals in your family as well as those people in your social circle.

Those with strong online social networks might consider fundraising online as a way to generate cash. If you take that approach, a good idea to consider is to send two separate notices: a more intimate and personalized "update" message to family, and a different (but still warm) direct fundraising appeal to your social media connections. In case you don't know, it's relatively easy to ask people for money via the Internet. Sites like Edulender and Sponsor My Degree let you create free online profiles and then your friends, family, and even total strangers can donate dollars to help you reduce college costs or avoid debt.

Any funding you can amass — whether it's from birthday funds, cash for the holidays or perhaps money given to you for high school graduation — will be dollars you can put toward higher education. Those monies directly translate into less student loan debt.

What about older students who might be considering going to graduate or professional school, but want to avoid massive student loan debt? If you fall into that category, there is one good alternative to pay for higher education costs as well, without borrowing. That alternative resource is your employer.

For those who are working, begin by seeking out employer-paid educational benefits. Obviously, these programs are geared toward those who earn a steady paycheck, but want to get a degree by attending school at night, on the weekend, or on a part-time or full-time basis.

Under any of these scenarios, your firm can pay for some or all of your tuition upfront, or your employer may reimburse you for certain college-related expenses.

Under federal tax law, you can receive up to $5,250 a year in tuition assistance from your employer. Best of all, you don't have to report the money as income to the IRS.

So what's the catch? The "catch" is that the money has to be used for classes or education that would further your skills in your *existing* line of work. You can't get favorable tax treatment if an employer pays for classes that would qualify you for a new, different career.

You might also be wondering why a company would foot the bill for your education anyway? Many employers use education assistance programs as a recruitment tool or as a way to retain good workers.

Besides, under Section 17 of the federal tax code, which was made permanent in 2013 tax legislation, employers are allowed to take tax deductions for providing educational benefits to employees.

Separately, if you are a working parent and your child is a stellar student — let's say a National Merit Scholar — some companies will automatically pay for at least part of his or her undergraduate tuition as a benefit to you, the employee.

* * *

So let's assume that you've truly exhausted all your other financing options. Now it's time to look at borrowing, starting with the tried-and-true strategy of knowing your borrowing limits

Set Borrowing Limits and Stick to Them

As previously mentioned, there's no universal agreement on how much debt is "reasonable" or how much student loan debt is "excessive." But college pros do offer insights into how to evaluate potential borrowing, and how to avoid going overboard with student loans.

College expert Lucie Lapovsky says she'd rather see students take on some debt if it means they can work less while in school and get through college as quickly as possible. "The data show that students are less likely to finish college if they go to school less than full time," she says.

Lapovsky is referring to a concept known as "intensity," which refers to the amount of effort and time you put toward your schooling. Long story short, students with more "intensity" — i.e. those who take a full load while in school — tend to have better educational outcomes than those who go only part-time and have less "intensity."

Lapovsky's suggestion: "Take 18 or 21 hours a term, go year round, and try to get out in three years."

"Even if you have to go into $20,000 to $30,000 worth of debt overall, the extra money you'll make a year sooner out of college will give you a higher rate of return and also improve your chances of college completion," she says.

What she doesn't advocate, however, is taking out massive amounts of student loans at schools that you clearly can't afford. Lapovsky cites New York University as a campus that is "notorious for giving out poor aid packages. There are lots of stories about students there taking out $50,000 a year in loans. That's ridiculous," she says.

But $20,000 to $30,000 in debt, she argues, "is not too much to worry about."

"This is your investment in human capital that's going to last you a lifetime," she says.

When her daughter, Nicole, got a full-ride to NYU, Judith Manigault considered it a true blessing.

"It still brings tears to my eyes any time I even think about it — especially because of what we were going through financially at the time," Manigault says. "I was just believing God. I said 'This is a bright girl. You've got to do something for her.' Fortunately, NYU came through with the full deal, and it was the only school in New York City where my daughter applied."

Obviously, Manigault's daughter was a "perfect fit" for NYU. But regardless of what school you aim to attend, or are already attending, you can lower potential debt by setting borrowing limits in other ways.

Rather than capping your loans at an arbitrary dollar figure, some experts suggest instead that you tie your borrowing limit to your future income.

"A good rule of thumb is to not have more debt than what you expect your first year salary is going to be," says Kalman Chany. Just be careful not to over-estimate your initial pay, as many college grads are apt to do. Unfortunately, until many students get into the "real world" they tend to over-estimate their beginning salary, and under-estimate their total bills. So take your overall finances into account when considering how much debt is prudent to carry and what your total monthly obligations are likely to be after graduation.

Always Get Federal Loans First

If you take on student loan debt for college, there are two types of loans: federal loans and private loans. You always want federal loans first because these loans usually have fewer fees, lower interest rates, and more flexible options, such as better loan forgiveness and loan deferment plans.

Congress sets the interest rates on federal student loans annually. As of this writing, undergraduate loans first disbursed between July 1, 2014 and June 30, 2015 carried fixed interest rates of 4.66%. Direct unsubsidized loans for graduate students currently carry a 6.21% rate. And for Direct PLUS loans, which are available to parents or graduate students, the fixed loan rate is 7.21%. Again, these rates change each year. So if you're reading this as of July 1, 2015 or later, be sure to double-check for the most up-to-date rates.

With federal student loans, you can choose from four general loan repayment plans:

- **The 10-year standard repayment plan**. This is the one that all borrowers are automatically enrolled in by the Department of Education. This plan requires you to repay your college debt in equal installments starting six months after you've graduated or left school.
- **The 10-year graduated repayment plan**. This plan also gives you a decade to repay your college debts. However, your payments start out very low and then rise every two years, based on the assumption that your starting salary will be modest but your income will increase over time.
- **The extended repayment plan**. This option lets you stretch out your student loan payments for as long as 25 years, and you can make fixed or graduated payments.
- **An income-related repayment plan**. Within this category, there are three options, each of which has a payment term ranging anywhere from 10 to 25 years:
  - **Income-based repayment**, which is based on your income and family size, and caps the amount of your monthly student loan payment.

- o **Income-sensitive repayment**, which is tied to your salary. When you pay goes up, your student loan repayments rise; if your pay falls, so does your student loan payment.
- o **Income-contingent repayment**, which is based on factors including your salary your spouse's income, and your family size. This plan is also only for those with direct PLUS loans (Parent Loans for University Students), graduate student loans, and direct subsidized and unsubsidized loans, such as Stafford Loans.

The main "drawback" of federal student loans is also, in some regards, an "advantage" — because the federal government imposes loan limits. Dependent students are currently limited to taking out a total of $31,000 in and independent students can borrow no more than $57,000 in total federal student loans. These limits represent a "drawback" to the extent that federal loans may not be sufficient to cover your financial needs, which is one reason why many students also turn to private loans. But caps on federal loans may also serve a positive purpose, by keeping some borrowing in check.

Jaclyn Vargo, the Harvard alumna with the ice skating background, urges students to think long and hard before going into debt for college regardless of whether they take on federal or private student loans.

"The more loans you have, it's like being in a financial prison," she says. "The best asset you can give to yourself is minimal student loans. So go to an affordable school and do really, really well there."

The idea of debt being a financial "prison" may seem far-fetched to some. But just visit the websites for the Consumer Financial Protection Bureau or ProjectOnStudentDebt.org — where borrowers describe the toll that college debt has taken on their health, personal relationships, careers and their finances — and you'll see why student loans are increasingly trapping college grads and making them feel "imprisoned" in numerous ways.

Understand All Your Loan Options

Taking the time to understand what types of loans are available, and what your responsibilities are for paying back those loans, can help you make the most informed decisions about financing your college education.

There are several different types of federal student loans: Direct Subsidized and Direct Unsubsidized Loans; Direct PLUS Loans; and Federal Perkins Loans.

Thanks to government legislation passed in 2013, there is currently a cap on federal student loan rates at 8.25% for undergraduate Stafford loans, 9.5% for graduate Stafford loans and 10.5% for Direct PLUS loans.

Federal PLUS Loans let parents or graduate students borrow for college. Parents must have decent credit to get a PLUS loan and repayment begins 60 days after the last disbursement of the loan. The repayment period can last up to 10 years. Interest and principal may also be deferred in some circumstances. Since PLUS loans are based solely on good credit, a parent's income and personal debt are not factors in the loan approval process. There are obvious pros and cons to this, especially if a parent takes on more loans than advisable. In such a scenario, the burden of those financial loans can rest on both a student's and a parent's shoulders. What's more, other relatives may be indebted as well, since a parent can also obtain a credit- worthy co-signer in order to obtain a PLUS loan. If you contemplate doing this, be upfront about the risks of co-signing a student loan or asking someone else to do so. If the loan isn't repaid for any reason, whoever signed for the loan will be liable and will face collection activity, as well as severe financial and credit consequences.

Your financial aid package will outline what loans you qualify for. You may also be eligible for private student loans, but realize that these are typically more expensive than federal student loans. They also often feature variable interest rates, making your payments less predictable over time.

Key Differences Between Federal and Private Student Loans

Some of the key differences between federal and private student loans are listed below.

Repayment requirements — federal student loans don't need to be paid until six months after you graduate, leave school, or change your enrollment status. Private student loans typically have to be repaid while you are still in school.

Interest rates — interest rates are fixed on federal student loans are usually much lower than private student loan rates. Also, some federal loans are subsidized loans, where the government pays the interest on the loan while you're in school. Private student loans are not subsidized so you are responsible for paying all the interest on the loan.

Credit checks — you won't need a credit check for a federal loan, but private student loans will require you to have a good credit score and a clean credit report.

Cosigner — federal student loans typically don't require a cosigner; most private student loans do have this requirement.

Tax advantages — interest on federal student loans may be tax-deductible; interest on private loans typically is not tax-deductible.

Consolidation options — federal student loans can be consolidated into a Direct Consolidation Loan; you don't have this option with private loans.

Repayment options — if you end up struggling to make your loan payments on a federal loan, you may be able to reduce your monthly payment or postpone loan payments temporarily. Most private lenders don't offer as many types of loan deferment or forbearance options, so these loans are less flexible in repayment terms.

Prepayment penalty fees — federal loans don't impose a penalty fee for paying off the loan before the loan term. Private loans can impose prepayment penalty fees, so be sure to review the terms carefully.

Loan forgiveness — if you work in public service — say you are a police officer, social worker or a nurse — you may be eligible to have a portion of your federal loans forgiven. Lenders typically don't offer any type of loan forgiveness program for private loans.

Loan assistance — you can get free help for federal loans by calling 1-800-4-FED-AID and review information on the U.S. Department of

Education website. Recently, the federal government announced plans to oversee private lenders. As part of that effort, there will be an advocate for borrowers with private loans. To reach this advocate, you will need to contact the Consumer Financial Protection Bureau's private student loan ombudsman.

Pay a Little Along the Way

As mentioned, federal loans may be subsidized, meaning the government is paying the interest on those loans while you're in school. This helps you avoid accruing interest during the years before you graduate. But recognize that with unsubsidized federal loans, and with private loans, you don't get that subsidy. So if you don't make student loan payments immediately after getting those loans, the interest gets capitalized — or added to — your original student loan balance. This is how students who borrow, say $20,000 over four years, wind up having a total student loan debt closer to $27,000 by the time they graduate from school.

To avoid seeing all that interest accrue, the smart strategy is to pay a little at a time — at least on unsubsidized loans — right after you take them. At a minimum, pay the interest on those loans so that it doesn't pile up unnecessarily, adding to your post-graduation student loan debt.

Stay Out of Default

Once you graduate, leave school, or drop below half-time enrollment, you have a six-month grace period before you are required to begin repaying your student loans. During this grace period, your loan servicer should send you payment information advising you when your first monthly payment is due. Don't ignore that notice! If you do, you could set yourself up for falling into delinquency and ultimately into default with your student loans.

When you miss one or more student loan payments, your loan will become delinquent. But if you don't make your monthly student loan payments for 270 days, the loan goes into "default" status. At this point, the federal government has the right to hold on to any federal tax refunds you are supposed to get, and can also garnish up to 15% of your net income. Whenever your loan falls into a default status, it will also be noted on your credit report, hurting your credit score.

Clearly, you want to avoid ever getting into that situation. So here are seven practical and effective ways to pay off your federal and private student loans — and stay out of default.

1. **Choose the shortest repayment plan you can afford**

   While it's tempting to want to stretch out your student loan payments in the short run, in order to lower your monthly note, that can be a costly strategy in the long run. The longer you have your student loans in repayment, the more interest you're paying.

   So pick the *shortest* repayment term that you can reasonably afford and make extra payments whenever possible. The goal is to pay down that student loan debt quickly so that you don't have to carry that debt for more than 10 years. That may not always be possible, but try to avoid automatically choosing the *longest* repayment period offered.

2. **Talk to your employer.**

   Some employers offer student loan payoff programs as a benefit to employees. This might be conditional, in that you agree to work for that employer for a certain number of years to be eligible for the full benefit.

   Student loan assistance programs can be very valuable if you intend on working for the same employer for a few years. Find out if your company offers student loan assistance programs and what the qualification requirements are — you just might be able to pay off that student loan by being a loyal employee.

3. **Look into the Federal Student Loan Repayment Program.**

   If your first job out of college — or even your second or third gig — is with the government or a federal agency, you may be eligible for student loan repayment benefits.

   If you have federal student loans and work for a federal agency, find out if you are eligible for the Federal Student Loan

Repayment Program that is administered by the Office of Personnel Management.

The program allows employees of a federal agency to have federal loans paid off, up to $10,000 per year, up to a maximum of $60,000. Visit the Office of Personnel Management website at www.opm.gov to learn about your options.

4. **Seek out a loan deferment, forbearance, or cancellation if you can't make payments**
When you are dealing with economic hardship, you may qualify for a loan deferment or forbearance. In some cases, you can have your loans canceled altogether.

For instance, Sallie Mae offers deferments for nearly 20 different types of life situations that have left the borrower in a state of economic hardship or financial distress.

If you become unemployed, are a new mother re-entering the workforce, volunteer for a non-profit, a military enlistee, or meet other eligibility requirements, you might qualify for a loan deferment. In all of these situations, simply having your loan payments postponed can provide significant financial relief.

You might be able to have your monthly payments reduced if you've been through a divorce, got into a car accident, or have dealt with other life situations that have left you in financial distress.

Also, if you are enduring a lengthy medical illness that has a significant and chronic impact on your financial situation, the Department of Education may be able to cancel your federal loans entirely so that you are no longer in student loan debt.

Don't be afraid to explore your options so that you can stay on a healthy financial track. You can fill out the two-page Statement of Financial Status on the Department of Education's website here.

5. **Consider the extra benefits of volunteering and your career path**
If you volunteer at AmeriCorps, VISTA, or the Peace Corps, or you volunteer for any organization that helps people in underserved communities, you can have your student loans canceled completely.

You might also qualify for student loan benefits based on your career path. Many working professionals such as police officers, doctors, nurses, teachers, lawyers, and healthcare professionals also qualify for loan forgiveness programs and outright cancellations.

So find out if you might be eligible to have your student loans canceled or forgiven based on your volunteer activities and contributions, or your profession.

6. **Negotiate loan terms**

You may be able to negotiate loan rates and terms on any certain private student loans you acquire.

You can ask for a lower interest rate under certain conditions, such as allowing payments to be automatically deducted from your checking or savings account, making a set number of payments on time, earning good grades, or by qualifying for any other incentive programs the lender offers.

Here's an example of one good incentive program. In 2014, Discover Student Loans launched a unique new program called "1% Cash Reward for Good Grades." The initiative gives a cash reward to undergraduates and grad students who earn a minimum 3.0 grade point average. The cash reward is paid out in the form of a check and is equal to 1% of the loan amount of each new Discover student loan.

Students are eligible for the reward if they submit an application for a Discover Undergraduate, Health Professions, Law, MBA or Graduate student loan from May 1, 2014 on, and then achieve a 3.0 or better GPA during the academic term covered by the loan. Eligible students must also redeem their reward within six months after the end of the academic term covered by the loan. This cash reward program will continue into 2015 and beyond.

"Discover's new 1% Cash Reward for Good Grades aligns with our philosophy of providing support and giving back to our customers. We are offering an incentive and reward to students who study hard, earn good grades and make an investment in their future," says Danny Ray, president of Discover Student Loans. "We strive to help families and students with their educational goals by assisting them every step of the way, whether through understanding the loan process, finding scholarships, or rewarding students for a job well done."

The new 1% Cash Reward for Good Grades is part of Discover's goal of providing responsible options to help students pay for college and graduate school. Discover is very unique among private lenders in that all Discover Student Loans have zero fees — including no origination fees, zero prepayment fees, and no late payment charges or returned payment fees, either.

7. **Be careful with student loan consolidation programs.**
   You've probably already received offers in the mail to consolidate your student loans for a low rate. The biggest benefit of consolidating your student loans is a lower monthly payment, but choosing to reduce your payments could mean you carry that debt for *decades* to come.

   If you decide to consolidate your student loans, make sure you understand all the terms and conditions of the agreement.

   Regardless of the program you choose, you will still have to keep your private and federal loans separate. Be careful about which loans you roll into a larger loan because some loans offer more benefits and loan repayment options that you miss out on if you choose to consolidate.

   To figure out your best strategy for federal loans, visit the Department of Education's consolidation site at www.loanconsolidation.ed.gov, which is currently being phased into a new site, http://www.StudentLoans.gov.

   Student loan debt is one of the biggest financial responsibilities for many young adults, and meeting that monthly obligation can feel overwhelming at times.

   However, carrying student loan debt doesn't have to be a burden — and you certainly don't have to go into default — when you create a realistic payoff plan.

   Many people don't realize that they have several options for student loan repayment, or that they may even qualify for a loan deferment or loan cancellation. But these options certainly exist, and they're often yours for the asking.

* * *

College planning isn't easy. Nor is paying for higher education if the money has to come out of your own pocket or if you need to borrow funds for school.

But now that you've read *College Secrets*, you are light-years ahead. You now know how to cut costs, save money, and get all the aid you need from other sources to help fund a college education. Hopefully, your newfound knowledge will also help you graduate debt free — or at least with a minimal amount of college debt.

Now the rest is up to you. If you implement the tips, tricks and strategies I've shared throughout *College Secrets*, I guarantee that you will:

- Greatly ease the financial stress that goes with college planning
- Eliminate the need to rack up big credit card bills, sacrifice retirement, mortgage a home, or obtain unnecessary student loans to pay for college
- Avoid the numerous economic pitfalls and costly mistakes made by students and parents who are engaged in college preparation or financial planning; and
- Save $20,000 to $200,000 over the course of a four-year education!

I wish you and your family much success as you navigate the college maze … I know you can do it!

Best Wishes!

Lynnette Khalfani Cox,
The Money Coach

𝒥NDEX

CPSIA information can be obtained at www.ICGtesting.com
Printed in the USA
BVOW04s0612240914

367588BV00001B/1/P

9 781932 450118